⌘ If you or someone you know struggles with depression, I recommend *Get a Grip on Depression*. With years of experience as a therapist and minister, John helps you understand the nature of depression and helps you overcome it using proven principles from modern psychology and the Bible. John's practical approach is fresh and easy to use.

Dr. Kevin Leman, New York Times Bestselling
Author of *Have a New You by Friday*

⌘ Life is about change and life can be hard. Constant pressure can lead some people to give up. John Thurman is an expert on finding new hope and his book, *Get a Grip on Depression,* has proven answers about taking responsibility to create positive change. If you, or someone you care about, is battling depression, this is the book for you!

Dwight Bain, Nationally Certified Counselor,
Certified Life Coach, Best-selling author

⌘ There has never been a time in our history when people are under as much stress or there has been so much hopelessness. John's book, *Get a Grip on Depression*, will certainly bring light to the darkness of depression and help all who read it find hope.

Andrew Horner, Founder and Chief Servant
Officer, Premier Designs, Inc.

❖ *Get a Grip on Depression* is a balanced approach to battling the blues. It is biblically solid and psychologically sound. I thank my friend John Thurman for writing a book that will help and heal many people.

Dr. Charles Lowery, President of the
Lowery Institute for Excellence

⌘ *Get a Grip on Depression* is a refreshing, practical look at how to understand and manage depression by identifying "Stinking Thinking Patterns" and enhancing resilience through powerful principles found in God's Word. A great resource for pastors, counselors, and coaches.

Georgia Shaffer, Christian Life Coach, author of *Coaching the Coach* and PA licensed psychologist.

∽

⌘ In this life changing, mind altering book, John Thurman gives the reader the greatest gift in the world—the gift of hope. Apart from the name of Jesus, there is no word more beautiful than the word hope. It is the cure for depression and the reason for living. Biblically and practically John shows you the way out of the hopeless pit you find yourself in.

Gayle Rogers Foster (daughter of the late Adrian Rogers) and Senior Leader for Premier Designs

∽

⌘ I have known John for decades. Not only is he my friend, but he is a wise counselor. John shares from his heart truths that will transform your life. He will help you one step at a time to become the person God created you to be.

Todd Cook, Senior Pastor, Sagebrush Church, Albuquerque, NM

∽

⌘ For any of you who have been depressed or have friends or family who are depressed, this book is for you. It is designed to help you or your friend have a happy tomorrow.

Florence Littauer, International Speaker and Best Selling Author of *Personality Plus* and *Silver Boxes*.

∽

⌘ John Thurman helps you understand the devastating impact depression can have on you as a person, your relationships, and your career. Recent studies demonstrate that adults who are at risk for developing depression can benefit from a deep connection to their faith. In *Get a Grip on Depression*, John combines over thirty-five years of counseling experience integrating proven clinical principles with the timeless truths of Scripture to help you push back depression.

Bob VandePol, MSW, President,
Pax Crisis Response

⊰

⌘ *Get a Grip on Depression* is an excellent resource for anyone who has wrestled with the darkness of depression. Using the Bible as a source book, John's book is filled with practical tools to help remove the mystery of depression and then move forward with hope. I recommend it as a guide for anyone who works with or lives with someone who struggles to overcome this disease.

Gerry Wakeland, President,
CLASSEMINARS, Inc.

⊰

⌘ *Get a Grip on Depression* offers timely and powerful hope to people who struggle with depression and to those who love them. John Thurman is one of those rare people whose expertise as a counselor is matched by a profound understanding of Scripture and a heart that is genuinely compassionate. This unique combination comes through in the pages of his book. This book promises to be a valuable resource to de-stigmatize depression and direct a pathway to healing. As a pastor, I am grateful for this book and recommend it to pastors, counselors, and particularly those whose lives have been touched by this difficult journey.

R. Marshall Blalock, Pastor, First Baptist
Church of Charleston, SC

⊰

⌘ This remarkable book is essential reading in resiliency and mental toughness for everyone. This book is for anyone who is troubled by depression, anyone with loved ones fighting depression, any caregiver or pastor called to help those with depression, or any individual who wants to increase his or her own personal resiliency and mental toughness. A unique and essential approach to a vital topic.

Dave Grossman, LTC and author of
On Combat* and *On Killing

✑

⌘ Depression can be a dream stealer. *Get a Grip on Depression* combines the timeless truths of Scripture and proven principles that John has developed in over thirty-five years of practice. John Thurman is not only a professional counselor but a man who understands entrepreneurship. If you have been sidelined or slowed down by depression and want to recapture your dreams, this book can help.

Dr. Tom Barrett
Speaker and Author

✑

⌘ We have known John Thurman as an effective communicator for the past 20-plus years. He is wise, powerful, and delivers a clear message while speaking from his head and heart. His book, *Get a Grip on Depression,* can help you get a grip on life!

Greg & Melissa Terrell, Executive Directors,
Premier Designs Jewelry

Get a Grip
on
Depression

Get a Grip
on
Depression

John Thurman

©John Thurman, 2014

ISBN# 9780991284221
Library of Congress LCCN Control Number 2014936928
Published in the United States of America.

Bold Vision Books
PO Box 2011
Friendswood, Texas 77549
www.boldvisionbooks.com

Interior design by kae Creative Solutions
Edited by Katie McDivitt
Cover Photo by John Thurman

Dedication

༄

This book is dedicated to my parents, J.H. "Howdy" Thurman and Mary Anne Thurman who prayed for me, parented me, and who pointed me to faith.

To my wife of over forty years, Angie, who has been by my side as we have lived, loved, and faced life's challenges and blessings together.

To my children, J.S., Hannah, and their wonderful spouses, Satenik and Cory, and our grandsons Connor and Elijah.

Contents

Acknowledgments

The concept for *Get a Grip on Depression* is rooted in a segment of 2 Thessalonians 2:15, "Stand firm and keep a strong grip on the teaching we passed on to you."

This book is the result of a lifetime of helping people and could not have been accomplished without a lot of people helping me.

First and foremost, I am thankful to the Lord for His leadership and direction.

I am thankful for my parents who were readers, encouragers, infusers of hope, and a couple who expressed their love of God through a lifetime of community service.

I am appreciative for the things I learned at the North Carolina Outward Bound School, "To serve, to strive, and not to yield." As I look back over the past forty-plus years, that kernel of truth about resilience never left my mind.

I am grateful to my wife, Angie, who helped push me to get this project done. Much of what is shared in this resource has been experienced by both of us as we have lived life together.

Next, I want to acknowledge some of the mentors in my life who have inspired and cheered me along the way in my journey of faith.

Gay Hatcher, my spiritual grandmother, encouraged me to fall in love with Jesus and His Word. My early spiritual development was greatly influenced by her honest, upbeat, godly influence.

Lifelong friends Sib and Agnes Sexton, as well as Jim and Martha Farley, were key players as Angie and I grew, both as a couple and as followers of Christ, in our college days.

Harold and Deborah Bullock challenged me to think globally about the gospel and to look at practical ways to share the good news in "real life" situations.

I want to acknowledge the influence of Florence Littauer, who has gently nudged me to write for years. I deeply and profoundly appreciate her friendship and influence.

LTC David Grossman, (US Army, retired), whose speaking and writing have helped me develop a deeper understanding of resilience.

Thanks to the faculty and leadership of CLASSeminars, who have motivated me to carry on with this project.

Thank you to my fellow therapists and the staff at Christian Therapy Services, who have prayed for and with me while providing sound counsel and a great deal of input into this work.

Thanks to friends Andy and Joan Horner, founders of Premier Designs Jewelry, whose godly example and encouragement as Christian business leaders have enriched my life and family for over twenty years.

Thanks to Senior Pastor Todd Cook and the staff of Sagebrush Church, who have graciously provided a framework for me to develop this resource through the Living Free ministry.

I am humbled by and thankful for all of the men and women who have allowed me to come alongside them in their dark days of depression, to help them get a grip on their emotions, and learn how to live a purpose-filled, intentional life, even while pushing back this terrible condition.

And finally, thank you to the men and women of the Armed Forces who constantly stand watch over our nation. These men and women have modeled many of the truths I share in this book. To my sheepdog friends, thank you for your encouragement on this project.

God Bless.

John H. Thurman Jr. M.Div, M.A., LPCC
Professional Counselor, Author, and Crisis Response Specialist
Proverbs 3:5-6

Psalm 77:1-12

I cry out to God; yes, I shout.

Oh, that God would listen to me!

When I was in deep trouble,

I searched for the Lord.

All night long I prayed, with hands lifted toward heaven,

but my soul was not comforted.

I think of God, and I moan,

overwhelmed with longing for his help. Interlude

You don't let me sleep.

I am too distressed even to pray!

I think of the good old days,

long since ended,

when my nights were filled with joyful songs.

I search my soul and ponder the difference now.

Has the Lord rejected me forever?

Will he never again be kind to me?

Is his unfailing love gone forever?

Have his promises permanently failed?

Has God forgotten to be gracious?

Has he slammed the door on his compassion? Interlude

And I said, "This is my fate;

the Most High has turned his hand against me."

But then I recall all you have done, O Lord;

I remember your wonderful deeds of long ago.

They are constantly in my thoughts.

I cannot stop thinking about your mighty works.

—NLT

These words, written thousands of years ago by a man dealing with depression, though ancient, are contemporary. As you read the text, you feel his despair, hopelessness, problems with sleep, concentration, feelings of withdrawal, and isolation. In addition, the psalmist is angry with God. Though this psalm is a synopsis of this man's depression, we see the full circle of depression and recovery. Ultimately, the writer of this psalm was able to move from depression and despair to a sense of renewed hope.

It is my sincere hope that *Get a Grip on Depression* will give you up-to-date information, knowledge, practical help, and offer a way for you to learn how to manage and recover from depression. May this book become a part of your growing tool kit to assist you in managing and overcoming depression and other mood disorders.

Introduction

The purpose of *Get a Grip on Depression* is to help you better understand depression and to learn proven, effective ways to manage depression using a combination of the latest research and the ancient, but still relevant, principles of Scripture. Practically speaking, this workbook is designed to help you:

- ❖ Boost your mood naturally
- ❖ Understand the cause of depression
- ❖ Lower the risk and impact of depression
- ❖ Review meaningful stories and principles from Scripture
- ❖ Overcome mild depression
- ❖ Increase a sense of purpose, well-being, and mission
- ❖ Supplement your depression treatment
- ❖ Prevent relapse
- ❖ Relieve the residual symptoms of major depression
- ❖ Incorporate biblically-based, spiritual practices to alleviate and reduce the impact of depression

You've heard the old saying, "Insanity is doing the same thing repeatedly and expecting a different outcome." Maybe it's time to stop doing the same old thing.

This resource will offer a fresh perspective to depression. Some readers may believe this approach is too indirect and not "clinical" enough. My encouragement to you is to remember that depression constricts your opinion of your capabilities and keeps you in a comfort zone of low and slow. *Get a Grip on Depression* is about trying something a little different. If you are currently being treated with medication or counseling, then please continue. This resource will supplement the hard work you are already doing.

Medication and appropriate talk therapy help relieve the symptoms of depression up to 80 percent of the time for those who pursue treatment, but millions of Americans will never seek treatment.

One of the principles for getting a grip on depression is personal responsibility, which simply means you are an active player in your personal recovery. It is important for us to focus on responsibility and to be forward-looking. Seeing ourselves as perpetual victims of childhood or adult trauma tends to make us a prisoner of the past and gnaws at our sense of responsibility. All successful counseling has two things in common: It is forward-looking, and it requires assuming personal responsibility.

Here are some proven tips for getting the most benefit from using this resource:

First, choose to shift into a "growth mindset." Dr. Carol Dweck, author of *Mindset*[1], spent her life researching the origins of mindsets, their role in motivation and self-regulation, and their impact on achievement and interpersonal processes. Her findings give us two options, a growth mindset or a fixed mindset. Her research mirrors the teaching in the book of James about being double-minded. The Bible contains numerous other passages that deal with managing our thoughts.

A fixed mindset is one in which you believe you are born with a certain set of talents, abilities, and intelligence—all of which are unchangeable. Some people with a fixed mindset may find it more difficult to experience life change and growth. As a result, a fixed-mindset person fails to develop his abilities and is more likely to give up or become distracted and feel depressed when he fails to make the grade in his own eyes.

A person with a growth mindset begins in a different place. When you have a growth mindset you see yourself and others as more flexible, adaptable, and hopeful. Way down inside, you see the potential for growth and development. With the right motivation, effort, moral compass, and concentration you believe you can become better at almost anything. A person who has a growth mindset doesn't take failure so personally. That individual tends to see failure as an opportunity for growth. If one path doesn't work, then the person will try another.

As a Christian therapist, I believe that the Bible continually teaches the benefit of being growth-minded. I believe God is active in time, space, and history and that He has an active, life-fulfilling purpose for each of us. The Bible gives us truth, hope, and stories of those who have gone before us and have found such purpose.

From my own struggle with depression, I know that working toward a growth mindset in the middle of depression may seem close to impossible. But the truth found in the Bible is, "For I can do everything through Christ, who gives me strength" (Philippians 4:13 NLT). This confidence is not some magical incantation or mystical spiritual event, but it is a process or a journey.

The second benefit from this resource is to remember to do one thing at a time, one day at a time. The very nature of depression tends to slow you down and suck the life right out of you. Do you remember the funny and insightful movie *What About Bob?* from 1991? In the movie, the psychiatrist is portrayed by Richard Dreyfus and the patient by Bill Murray. Whenever the patient was having a bad day, the psychiatrist reminded him to "take baby steps." The movie advice is right. Pace yourself. Life change is done incrementally, over time. Dream big, develop a new vision for your life, but don't beat yourself up over setbacks.

Third, remember you are on a journey to reclaim the real you. Try to think about the days when you didn't feel so depressed. If you were normally sociable, you might want to put some time and effort into your relationships or engage in some type of non-electronic social activities. Don't get stuck in the humdrum grayness of depression. Mix it up if you are bored. Try some new activities or try some old activities that used to bring you joy.

Even when King David was in the pits of depression, wishing to die, feeling like he'd called dial-a-prayer and been put on hold, he remembered what God had done for him. When he wrote several of the psalms, his remembrance was the beginning of his recovery. Here are a few of those verses: Psalm 23:4, 32:7, 34:18, 43:56, 46:1, and 68:19.

Fourth, gently stretch yourself. You are in a marathon, not a sprint. As you continue to move out of the pit of depression, allow yourself a little bit of room to move out of the gray comfort zone.

Chapter 1

What is Depression?

Fred was a 34-year-old senior pastor serving his first church after faithfully serving as an associate pastor in a growing East Coast church. His wife and children were adjusting to the new town and a new church; all seemed to be going well. Fred enjoyed the work of the ministry. Teaching, preaching, and counseling were all aspects of the ministry that held significant meaning to him.

However, he was counseling a woman named Jill who was rather enamored with him. She was in her second abusive marriage. As Fred learned more about her history, he found out that Jill had never been in a safe relationship. She had recently returned to church when Fred became her pastor.

Fred believed the Lord was using him to help Jill. It started gradually, but Jill began to call Fred at the office and then at home, sometimes ten to fifteen times a day. Fred began to feel as if he was being stalked, so he informed her that he would no longer be able to work with her. He gave her a couple of referrals to therapists in the community. He also contacted the police, who could do nothing since anti-stalking laws were not yet established.

Fred and his family began to feel the pressure of her presence, but what could a pastor do with a church member like this? Fred had never encountered a similar situation. Since he was new to the area, he hadn't yet developed many relationships, so he contacted some minister friends from other areas who began to pray for him. Fred appreciated the support but continued to feel pressure from Jill's presence. His wife began to notice Fred was withdrawn and seemed blue most of the time. He was tired, not sleeping well, and feeling fatigued. Others also noticed that he seemed anxious and had a hard time concentrating.

Fred read a couple of articles about depression but did not think it could happen to him. After all, he thought he was one of God's servants, and it would not be right for a pastor to be depressed. One day it all came to a head as he stepped toward the pulpit. He felt the dark undertow of sadness and depression suck the life right out of his soul. He began to preach, and as he read from the Bible, he was overwhelmed and began to cry. The cry built into a sob, and then, to the horror of the congregation, he collapsed and had to be carried to the church foyer.

His wife and three children pulled into the parking lot as the medics loaded him into the ambulance. After a thorough exam by the emergency room physician, Fred was told he was dealing with a major depressive episode.

At this point, Fred confided in an older pastor that he needed help. This was a huge step for Fred, as he had previously equated receiving psychological counseling with being spiritually inferior. The older pastor referred Fred to a psychiatrist friend. Fred saw the doctor, got on a medical treatment plan, and within several weeks began to feel better. Within a number of months, he told his wife that he felt like he was finally coming out of the pit, or, as he put it, "the dark room began to lighten up a little."

Fred had experienced the overwhelming sense of despair and worthlessness that is common among people with a major depressive episode. With good medical management; a vibrant, transparent relationship with Christ; a commitment to the Word of God; and the close support of Christian friends, Fred was able to overcome depression.

Today, Fred serves a growing congregation as senior pastor and has been able to help hundreds of people who are living in the black hole of depression.

If people in our families, churches, and workplaces are going to be helped with depression, it is crucial that we understand some basic information about this disorder. Therapy and medication are effective in treating up to 80 percent of clinical depression cases.

Nearly everyone is familiar with the experience of feeling depressed, and moodiness is almost universal. Because these life experiences are so common, how do these normal reactions move into mood disorders such as depression?

Hippocrates was the first one to recognize melancholia as a medical illness. In the past, psychiatrists, psychologists, and therapists saw this clinical picture as measurably different than milder forms of depression. Melancholy lasts weeks or months during which time the individual suffers from despondency, irritability, and restlessness with a slowing down of mental processes and movement, diminished appetite, sleeplessness, and powerful suicidal urges as well as other debilitative symptoms.

In recent years the term "depression" has become more broadly defined and has led to a broad, ever-changing definition. Psychiatrists, psychologists, social workers, and therapists have long been taught that depression is a symptom, a syndrome, or a disorder.

Depression can be a serious medical condition that affects the body, mind, and spirit. It impacts the way one thinks about everything. A depressive disorder is not the same thing as feeling down or having a little case of the blues. It is not a sign of weakness or a condition to simply wish, will, or pray away. People with a depressive illness cannot simply "suck it up and get on with life." Without recognizing and treating depression, its symptoms can last for weeks, months, or even years. Ultimately, some who suffer from it commit suicide. The good news is there are a number of proven treatment options that alleviate or at least manage depression. These treatment options may include treatment with medication, talk therapy, nutrition, exercise, and even exercising spiritual disciplines.

How Common is Depression?

In my years of counseling, I've met men and women who have had one bout of depression after another, and others who have only had one depressive event. The number of people overwhelmed by depression increases annually, and depression has a powerful impact on families, churches, and businesses. In fact, in the past three decades, our country has experienced an epidemic of depression. While most of us may not have extended battles with depression, virtually no one is immune to it. We have imperfect personalities, which interact with an imperfect sinful world; therefore, all of us will have experiences with this emotion in some form or fashion.

People from every walk of life struggle with depression, including doctors, lawyers, teachers, factory workers, housewives, teenagers, the elderly, and even men and women in the ministry—maybe especially men and women in the ministry.

The Old Testament tells us that some of our great heroes of the faith struggled with depression. King David (Psalm 3, 40:1, 55:4), Elijah (1 Kings 19:5-8), and Jonah (Jonah 1 and 3) are three examples. The Bible study at the end of this book will reveal others who struggled.

Abraham Lincoln struggled with bouts of depression. During one of his darker days, he wrote to a friend, "I am now the most miserable man living. If what I feel were equally distributed to the whole human family, there would not be one cheerful face on the earth. Whether I shall ever be better, I cannot tell; I awfully forbode I shall not. To remain as I am is impossible; I must die or be better, it appears to me...."[2]

Mood disorders, (which include major depression, dysthymia—now called "persistent depressive disorder"), and bipolar disorder, affect 23.8 million American adults each year, which translates into one in 15 American adults.[3] Bipolar disorder annually affects 5.7 million American adults, or 2.6 percent of the population. A report issued by WebMD states that about 11 percent of Americans who are age twelve or older take antidepressants, including many who have not seen a mental health professional in the past year.[4]

The Center for Disease Control's National Center for Health Statistics reports that the rate of antidepressant use in the United States has increased nearly 400 percent since 1988.[5]

The Price of Depression

Depression can be called a disorder of superlatives.

It is the most common mental health disorder affecting Americans and is potentially the most lethal because some depressed people select suicide as the permanent solution to temporary problems. In my opinion, depression is the most debilitating of any other disorder because it impairs a person on so many levels, ranging from emotional and physical to social and financial.

The emotional drain is the most obvious. The grief, pain, despair, loss of hope and faith, and the seemingly lost potential for a higher quality of life are all heavy prices to pay.

Depression leads to illness and pain, which in turn leads to frequent trips to medical and counseling professionals. A person with depression may exhibit an unwillingness to maintain his health and an inability to follow recommended treatment, which may result in an untimely death.

Further, the direct cost of psychiatric treatment accounts for only a small part of the medical cost of depression. For various reasons, people with mood disorders spend twice the average amount on non-psychiatric medical treatment. Depression can mimic medical illness, and any illness feels worse to someone who is depressed. A person's health may deteriorate because of behaviors rooted in depression, such as the lack of nutrition and exercise, failure to comply with medical treatment because of passivity and pessimism, or because of an imbalance in hormonal and neurotransmitter activity.

Depression is one of the most widespread psychiatric disorders by any measure; only alcoholism and anxiety disorders may be more common. According to one major survey, approximately 26.2 percent of Americans who are age eighteen and older (about one-fourth of all adults) suffer from a diagnosable mental disorder in any given year.

Depression is not a one-size-fits-all disorder. It comes in various sizes and shapes. The definitions and the ways we treat depression will continue to evolve as we learn more about the nature of depression. In 2013, the American Psychiatric Association released the fifth edition of the *Diagnostic and Statistical Manual of Mental Disorders* (DSM-5), further helping us to add to our understanding and treatment of depression and the other two major mood disorders: persistent depressive disorder (formerly called dysthymia) and bipolar disorder. While some will experience different symptoms, and while some of the labels may seem too broad, they do help clinicians, pastors, and researchers study and exchange information about the countless faces of depression.

What is Major Depression?

Major depressive disorder, or major depression, is characterized by a combination of symptoms that interfere with a person's ability to work, sleep, study, eat, and enjoy once-pleasurable activities. Major depression is disabling and prevents a person from functioning normally. Some people may experience only a single episode within their lifetime, but more often a person may have multiple episodes.[6]

Depression hurts.

The DSM-5 lists the following symptoms of depression:

- ❖ Persistent, sad, or empty mood
- ❖ Loss of interest or pleasure in ordinary activities, including sex
- ❖ Decreased energy, fatigue, being slowed down
- ❖ Sleep disturbances (insomnia, early morning waking, or oversleeping)
- ❖ Eating disturbances (loss of appetite and weight, or weight gain)
- ❖ Difficulty in concentrating, remembering, making decisions
- ❖ Feelings of pessimism, hopelessness
- ❖ Feelings of guilt, hopelessness, worthlessness, and helplessness
- ❖ Thoughts of death or suicide; suicide attempts
- ❖ Irritability
- ❖ Excessive crying or weepiness

Along with items listed in the DSM-5, individuals also report chronic aches and pains that don't respond to treatment. Others report pulling away from God while others become over-involved in spiritual things.

The symptoms of depression fall into four broad areas.[7]

Thinking. When you are depressed, your thought processes are different from when you are not depressed. Some people say their thought processes seem slowed down or muddled.

When you're depressed, you believe everything you touch, think, or do is going to fail. You even view your successes as failures. Your future looks bleak, and you credit this to your lack of talent. Hurdles that normally seem like little speed bumps turn into deep dark chasms.

A pessimistic explanatory style[8] is at the bottom of most depressed thinking, meaning you see the cause of your tragedies and your setbacks as pervasive, permanent, and personal.[9] You believe your setbacks will last forever, that they will subvert everything you do, and you are at fault.

Mood. When you are depressed, you feel terrible: sad, discouraged, and hopeless. Life has lost its zest. To quote Aerosmith, *you feel like your get up and go, got up and went.* When you feel depressed, sadness is not the only emotion you feel. Sadness invites its two friends, anxiety and irritability, to the party. They usually aren't far away. When the depression grows, anxiety and feelings of hostility slip away and the depressed person begins to feel numb and flat.

Behavior (passivity, indecisiveness, suicide). People who are depressed often cannot begin the most routine tasks, and give up easily when setbacks occur.

A writer has a hard time getting her first words written. When she finally does, she notices four misspelled words and does not touch her computer for a month. She has a hard time seeing alternatives, failing to realize she produced 1,500 words in one sitting.

A depressed youth pastor calls in an order for a personal pizza on his day off and when asked about toppings, he stares at his cell phone. Even such a simple choice is too overwhelming for him. After an awkward silence, he disconnects. As the choices of life begin to overwhelm the depressed person, he or she may begin to contemplate suicide.

Somatic concerns. The deeper the depression, the more your body bears, and the more it rebels. Appetite goes away because food has no taste and brings no comfort. Intimacy dwindles because closeness takes too much energy. Even sleep is affected; you either wake up too early or cannot get to sleep.

To be diagnosed with depression, you don't have to be showing symptoms in all of these areas, and no particular symptom is required. One thing is for certain, though: The more symptoms you have, and the more intense each one is, the more certain you can be that the problem is depression.

The truth is many people deny their depression. Until you own it, it will own you. As we get through these first few chapters, I will show you the way out. But before we get there, we have to know what we are dealing with.

In more than thirty-five years in the people-helping business, I have noticed that depression also dramatically affects one's spirituality. There are times when depression leads a person to pull away from God or causes a person to believe God has rejected him or her. In other instances, depression leads some people to become over-involved in spiritual activities.

Major Depression

Major depression is the most recognizable type of mood disorder. Major depressive disorder is a disabling condition that adversely affects a person's family, work, or school life, eating and sleeping patterns, and overall health. If major depression goes unchecked and untreated, it can leave a person feeling so empty and desperate that they might be at risk for choosing suicide as a permanent solution to a temporary problem. This desperation can be averted with treatment.

Case Study #1 - The Rancher

Bobby was a successful rancher and real estate developer in eastern New Mexico. He was the fourth generation to work his family's ranch, and he had a profitable development company that he ran with his wife, Sarah. Their three boys were doing in well in school, with two of them attending the University of New Mexico and the other one attending high school and participating on the calf-roping team.

Bobby and Sarah seemed to have it all—a great life, wonderful kids, and profitable business ventures. Then the 2008 downturn in the economy began to slowly reduce their resources. As Bobby watched his businesses and his family feel the impact of the downturn, he began to withdraw. In addition to withdrawing from his family, Sarah noticed he was beginning to drink more than his usual one or two beers on the weekend. She was also concerned about his increasingly sarcastic and negative tone.

Bobby continued to spiral into discouragement, despair, and ultimately depression. One afternoon he decided to check on his herd on the west side of the ranch. He got on his ATV, put his Ruger Mini-14™ in the rack, as he usually did, and headed out. As he drove, he took in the beautiful, expansive skies and broad horizons of New Mexico. In the distance he could see a storm brewing. He spotted two blue-white virgas (streaks of water drops or ice particles falling out of a cloud and evaporating before reaching the ground), and it looked like he would have the opportunity to experience another breathtaking New Mexico sunset.

He gazed at the sky, taking it all in. His last sunset, he thought. He had a good life insurance policy. The kids were set, and Sarah would be taken care of. She could unload the real estate development company and survive on the cash from the policy and the income from the ranch.

Bobby drove through the herd, noting that it had been a good calving season. The herd was healthy and the price of beef was going up. As he maneuvered through the cattle he did what every rancher does. He counted heads. He eventually got to a small rise and parked his ATV. He stepped out of the driver's seat and took it all in. In the distance, the blue-white virgas were turning gold. He glanced toward his house, which was about five miles away. Then he leaned back into the bright yellow seat of his John Deere Gator, reached for his rifle, and wondered what it would be like to end it all.

He drew in a deep, last breath and tearfully asked God to forgive him and take care of his family. He pulled the bolt back and felt the round slip out of the magazine into the chamber. Then as he heard the loud snap of the bolt locking the round into place, he heard a calf crying out.

"John, when that round locked in and the calf cried out, it's like the Lord was reminding me of the lost sheep story," he told me later. "Time stopped and I thought, *What am I doing?* Then I broke down and started to cry. After a few minutes I cleared my rifle, finished up my thermos of coffee, and headed back to the house. Sarah had no idea what had gone on, but I told her I needed some help. She gave me a long, intense hug and suggested we call our preacher. That is how I found out about you."

Bobby and I were able to work face to face and via Skype™. He gave me permission to talk with his family doctor who was able to get him some short-term, anti-depressant treatment. In addition, Bobby began reading *Unmasking Male Depression* by Dr. Archibald Hart, and Dr. Daniel Amen's book, *Change Your Brain, Change your Life*.

Bobby, Sarah, and their family were able to navigate through those dark days. The ranch is doing well now and the real estate business is slowly improving.

Major depression is what most people think of when they hear someone is struggling with depression, but this type of depression is only one manifestation in the depressive spectrum. Here are some other fairly typical types of depression.

Case Study # 2 – The Flight Medic

Sally was referred by a friend and member of IAVA (Iraq and Afghanistan Veterans of America). She'd met my friend at the VA hospital where both were being treated for wounds they'd received during Operation Enduring Freedom.

Sally had completed her second tour as a flight medic stationed at Fort Carson, Colorado, and had recently been honorably discharged after serving her country. She returned to New Mexico to get back into the real world and move on with her life.

On the first day we met, I went to the waiting area, picked up her chart, and introduced myself.

She said she was being treated for her post-traumatic stress disorder at the VA as well as receiving ongoing care for some shrapnel wounds she had received when a mortar round exploded near her medevac helicopter. Her primary reason for coming to me was to help with some recurring depression.

Over the next several months, she told me about her family legacy of service, her great-grandfather and a great-aunt who had served in World War II, a grandfather who served in Vietnam and the first Gulf War, and a brother who had attended the Air Force Academy and who was now serving as an officer in Air Mobility Command. She indeed had a grand legacy of service.

She had been on scores of missions as a flight medic with the Army. She had treated everything from a Marine with a broken leg as a result of a volleyball game to multiple amputees and had been a part of transporting the most precious cargo of all—"angels" (a common military slang for American soldiers killed in action).

She received excellent care at the VA, attended church, and was actively involved in a small-group Bible study mainly made up of IAVA members and friends. In addition, she took classes and hoped to one day become an emergency room doctor.

She understood the problems associated with overuse of psychotropic medications with service members and veterans, and she didn't want to misuse medications. Sally was tired of feeling like an "Ambien zombie" and wanted to look at some additional options for treating her depression, sleeplessness, and anxiety.

I referred her to Dr. Daniel Amen's work with veterans and National Football League players, specifically his work related to sub-types of depression and using nutraceuticals (targeted supplements), lifestyle changes, and medicine. She chose, with her doctor's less-than-enthusiastic support, to move off of her antidepressant and to a combination of supplements and lifestyle changes suggested on Dr. Amen's website. She did well with the transition, and her doctor was generally pleased with the results. She chose to stay on the Xanax for the panic attacks, though now she only needs them four to five times a month. She occasionally takes an Ambien but no longer feels like an Ambien zombie.

In our sessions, we chose to work on the combination of losses she'd experienced. She identified her concrete losses, abstract losses, imagined losses, and the most dreaded threatened losses. She began to understand that she was an incredibly strong woman who had lived more life and learned more about the things that matter in her two tours in Afghanistan than most folks do in a lifetime. She loved to quote Charles Dickens' *Tale of two Cities,* "It was the best of times, it was the worst of times." She learned how to manage the losses, feel the hurt and pain, as well as how to resist hopelessness and despair and become more resilient. She has continued to expand her horizons as a volunteer in her church and actively reaches out to other vets through her IAVA group. She is currently in her junior year at a university.

Minor Depression

Minor depression is characterized by having symptoms for two weeks or longer that do not meet full criteria for major depression.[10] Without treatment, people with minor depression are at high risk for developing major depressive disorder. Minor depression is often called a "situational depression," which is a prolonged episode of the blues that may be triggered by a loss or disappointment. Treatment may be required if the person does not seek and find relief for his or her depression after a reasonable period.

Case Study #3 - The School Teacher

Marcie felt as if she was in a time warp. Six months prior she had graduated with an elementary education degree from North Texas State University. Now she was a first-year teacher in the Municipal School District of Truth or Consequences, New Mexico, which was 150 miles from civilization, as she knew it. The area felt like another country. One of her best friends would always add "U.S.A." on any mail she sent Marcie. It was a joke, but it also made a point.

Marcie missed her family and friends, and she missed city life. "After all, once you have seen the Geronimo Springs Museum and eaten at the Dairy Queen, you have pretty much done everything you can do in T or C." She laughed as she told me the story. "The people are wonderful, but there is nobody in this town who is my age."

Marcie was going through a normal minor depression. She was homesick, missing her former life, and was not connected with anybody locally, except the parents of some of her students. If it wasn't for Facebook she said she'd have felt like a cloistered nun.

After a couple of sessions with Marcie, we both agreed that this was situational depression. With an action plan that included reaching out to others, she became more active in the community. We stayed in touch via email and telephone over the next few months. As Marcie began to understand more about her life transition, she began to post about some of the things she was learning about herself and about her relationship with the Lord on Facebook and Twitter with some of her friends who were going through the same thing, which gave her hope and comfort. She also got plugged into one of the local churches and began to build some new friendships and she set aside money in her budget for fun trips.

Minor depression, or situational depression, is usually short-term, annoying, and treated fairly easily. However, left unattended, it can turn into a deeper, more troublesome depression.

Psychotic Depression

Psychotic depression occurs when a person has severe depression, plus some form of psychosis, such as having disturbing false beliefs or a break with reality (delusions), or hearing or seeing upsetting things that others cannot hear or see (hallucinations).

Case Study #4 - The Medical Professional

Yolanda worked hard as a mother and as a medical program systems analyst for a large international company. Three weeks before her husband, Carlos, called me she had delivered her second child—a beautiful daughter. The delivery went well and within a couple of days, mom and baby were discharged. Shortly thereafter, Yolanda told Carlos she felt sad. He gave her a hug and tried to listen to and comfort her by letting her know he loved her and that she probably needed some rest. They pulled up the covers and went to sleep.

Around four in the morning, Yolanda woke up crying uncontrollably, screaming that she needed a knife and that she must sacrifice the baby. Carlos called 911. When the medics arrived and did their evaluation, Yolanda was transported to an emergency room, and then admitted to the hospital's psychiatric unit.

That evening Yolanda and I met for the first of many sessions over the next several months. Her psychiatrist diagnosed her with postpartum depression with psychotic features. Major life changes took a toll on her. The birth of her baby, the changes in her body, pressures at work, and the recent loss of her favorite grandmother put her in a bad place.

Over the coming months, through a combination of help from family and friends, therapy, and medication, Yolanda found her way back. Her marriage grew strong. She and Carlos enjoyed their little one. And her employer agreed to allow her to work part time as a telecommuter.

I recently ran into Yolanda and her family at the grocery store. She approached me with a huge smile on her face as she introduced me to her twelve-year-old daughter. As she hugged me, she lingered for a moment, whispering, "Thank you for helping me through a very dark time in my life."

Postpartum Depression

Postpartum depression (PPD) is a serious mental health problem characterized by a prolonged period of emotional disturbance, occurring at a time of major life change and increased responsibilities in the care of a newborn infant. PPD has significant consequences for both the new mother and her family. It is much more serious than the "baby blues" women experience after giving birth. A woman suffering from PPD experiences hormonal and physical changes in her body and that, combined with the new responsibility of caring for a newborn, is overwhelming.

Approximately one-half of all new mothers suffer from postpartum blues, a mild form of depression that commonly occurs a few days after childbirth. The new mother may find herself crying one minute, then feeling irritable the next. Some women have likened these feelings to premenstrual syndrome. In most cases, the symptoms disappear within two weeks and no medical treatment is required.

How Common is PPD?

An estimated 10 to 16 percent of postpartum women will experience PPD. Among women who have already experienced PPD following a previous pregnancy, some estimates increase to 41 percent.[11]

Its symptoms are much more intense than postpartum blues. The new mother may feel a sense of hopelessness and strong feelings of depression or anger. She may not be able to sleep, even when tired, or she sleeps most of the time, even when the baby is awake. She may experience a marked change in appetite. She may express extreme concern for the baby or lack of interest in the baby. She may also have suicidal urges or thoughts of harming the baby. If a woman suspects she is suffering from PPD, she should contact her physician immediately.

Case Study #5 - The Actress

Brook Shields seemingly has it all—happy marriage, celebrated beauty, critical applause, world fame. Yet after her child was born, she fought crippling postpartum depression.

After the birth of her child in 2003, the actress/model/icon was not singing lullabies in the pleasing voice that earned her rave reviews on Broadway. Nor was she learning to swaddle her newborn girl, Rowan Francis, named for her late father, Francis Shields. Instead, suffering from PPD, she found herself staring out of the window of her fourth-floor Manhattan apartment, contemplating putting an end to it all. But despite all she went through, Shields considers herself lucky.

"I was able to get help, and I was able to have a support system and recognize [the postpartum depression] relatively early," she says.

She also makes this key point with the clarity of hindsight, "Postpartum depression takes certain truths and turns them into the worst version of the truth. The truth is, your life changed forever when you have a child, but what you don't factor in is that it might be better and it might be more enriched."[12]

Seasonal Affective Disorder

Seasonal affective disorder (SAD) is characterized by the onset of depression during the winter months, when there is less natural sunlight. The depression generally lifts during spring and summer. SAD may be effectively treated with light therapy—which consists of daily exposure to bright, artificial light—but nearly half of those with SAD do not get better with light therapy alone. The symptoms include sleeping more than normal, weight gain, fatigue, headaches, irritability, and crying spells. These symptoms subside in spring and summer.

Although the exact cause of SAD has not been determined, research indicates that a malfunctioning of the body's biological clock because of shorter daylight hours might trigger it. Some believe that it is a form of hibernation. Light therapy fools the brain into supposing it is summer. The symptoms of SAD return, however, when the light therapy is discontinued.

The Mayo Clinic lists two variations of SAD.[13]

Winter-onset SAD symptoms include:

- ❖ Depression
- ❖ Hopelessness
- ❖ Anxiety
- ❖ Loss of energy
- ❖ Heavy, "leaden" feeling in the arms or legs
- ❖ Social withdrawal
- ❖ Oversleeping
- ❖ Loss of interest in activities you once enjoyed
- ❖ Appetite changes, especially a craving for foods high in carbohydrates
- ❖ Weight gain
- ❖ Difficulty with concentrating

Summer-onset SAD symptoms include:

- ❖ Anxiety
- ❖ Trouble sleeping (insomnia)
- ❖ Irritability
- ❖ Agitation
- ❖ Weight loss
- ❖ Poor appetite
- ❖ Increased sex drive[14]

Case Study #6 - The Radio Personality

Jackson hated winter in Minnesota. He moved there from Tucson earlier that year after being promoted to the position of drive-time disc jockey for a large FM radio network. He was a native South Westerner, but the promotion and pay increase were hard to turn down.

In late fall, he began to feel gloomy. He was having a hard time sleeping and an even harder time getting up. His morning show was beginning to suffer. Listeners were emailing and calling to say Jackson seemed a little off. Jackson went to his physician who put him on an antidepressant and referred him to a therapist who used light therapy along with traditional talk therapy. Jackson's symptoms improved immediately.

Over the last three years, Jackson has learned to manage his seasonal affective disorder. One of the ways he does it is by traveling back to Tucson when he can. He's thankful for the therapy he has received, telling me his show is consistently number one in his market.

Bipolar Disorder

Bipolar disorder is a serious brain illness. It is also called manic-depressive illness. People with bipolar disorder go through unusual mood changes. Bipolar is not the same as the normal ups and downs everyone goes through. Bipolar symptoms are more powerful than that. They can damage relationships and make it hard to go to school or keep a job. They can also be dangerous. Some people with bipolar disorder try to hurt themselves or attempt suicide.[15]

Sometimes people who suffer with the disorder feel happy and up and are much more active than usual. This is called mania. And sometimes people with bipolar disorder feel sad and down and are much less active. This is called depression. As the person's moods change, his or her energy and behavior change also.

During the manic phase of this illness, the person may become energetic, sleep little, and think and speak rapidly. Without treatment, a manic episode can last for weeks. A person in a manic phase also experiences at least three of the following symptoms:

❖ grandiose ideas or pumped-up self-esteem

❖ little need for sleep

❖ excessive talking

❖ increased activity that might be directed to accomplishing a goal or expressed as agitation

❖ a pleasure-seeking urge that might get funneled into sexual acting out

❖ overspending, or other ploys which often end in disaster

During the depressive phase, which is the more frequent form of the illness, the person is likely to lose interest in all activities and become completely withdrawn and lethargic. These symptoms may continue for months if a person doesn't seek treatment.

Between cycles, a person might feel normal for months or even years. Or he or she could experience faster mood swings (known as rapid cycling). Like depression, bipolar disorder takes on various forms.

Case Study #7 - The Reporter

Television journalist Jane Pauley made her network debut on NBC's *The Today Show* at the age of twenty-five. She went on to work for NBC's *Dateline* and later had her own talk show. At the age of fifty, Pauley began experiencing humiliating, confusing, bewildering episodes of depression and mania that characterize bipolar disorder. "The thing about my experience that I probably remember most vividly is that your self-perception is yanked out from under you and then you're left with no self-perception at all."[17]

Her story began in 2000 when she was being treated for chronic recurrent hives. Her skin erupted; doctors believe that the steroids used to treat her hives kick-started her bipolar disorder, which she may or may not have been genetically vulnerable to all along.

Once stabilized, she reintegrated back into her busy life. Pauley, always humble, is a much-needed role model for people with bipolar disorder. In a culture in which so few celebrities come forward and talk about their struggles with mental health issues, Pauley is a pioneer. She is a wonderful and dynamic example of someone with bipolar disorder who can still have success in her work, vocation, and life.[18]

She describes her experiences in her 2004 bestselling memoir, *Skywriting: A Life Out of the Blue*.

∽

Bipolar usually starts in early adulthood. It is equally common among men and women, although some variations strike one gender more than the other.[16] Women are more likely to experience major depression as their first episode and to have more depressive episodes overall. Men, on the other hand, typically experience manic episodes first and tend to have more of them than depressive cycles.

Bipolar disorder is a persistent illness. This disorder requires lifelong treatment, even during those seasons of life when a person is feeling good. Treatment is usually guided by a psychiatrist who is skilled in working with this condition. Your treatment team may include a psychiatrist, family doctor, nurse, and behavioral health therapist. The primary treatments for bipolar disorder include medications; individual, group, or family therapy; as well as educational and support groups. Ninety percent of those who have a single manic episode can expect to have a repeat experience. Suicide rates are higher in people who have bipolar disorder than in the general population. Successful treatment greatly reduces the frequency and intensity of episodes and reduces suicidal risks.

Now that we have a basic understanding of the different types of depression, you might be wondering if all depression is bad. In their book *Coping with Depression*, authors S. Y. Tan and J. Ortberg answer the question by explaining why people become depressed.

"Depression can be a purposive response, and its purpose is to help the person resolve an inner deadlock that is keeping him or her from functioning effectively; depression is productive when the deadlock is resolved and the person is able to move forward."[19]

Chapter 2

What Causes Depression?

If you listen to some reports today, it sounds like millions of people have become slaves to depression. While it is true that depression impacts millions of Americans, we get a sense that we've surrendered to the medical model that says depression is only caused by neurochemical imbalances and medication is the only way to treat it.

I am not opposed at all to medication. It can be a key to helping a person recover. However, when I look at a 400-percent increase in antidepressant prescriptions since 1988, I wonder if we are doing a better job of diagnosing mood disorders, or if we are only pushing medication at symptoms.

As we look into the causes of depression, it is important to note that there is a powerful connection between the way we think and the way we feel. Another powerful connection exists between the way we act and the way we feel. We will spend more time on this in later chapters. Those thoughts, feelings, and actions or behaviors enhance or restrict recovery. With that in mind, let's examine some of the typical causes of depression.

Three broad risk factors for depression exist. For clarity I will call them the three risk P's.

> ❖ Predisposing factors are the components of your background that increase your risk for depression. This includes your genetic makeup, upbringing, personal history, faith influences, culture, recent events, health,

diet, and other factors. Some of these you can change, others you cannot.

- ❖ Precipitating factors are the psychological, spiritual, emotional, and physical triggers that steer you into depression—such as stress, illness, and trauma.

- ❖ Perpetuating factors differ from the other two because they happen afterward. An example of this is a heavy drinker who uses alcohol as a means of coping with depression. The dominant effect of alcohol on the brain is also a cause of depression. Left unchecked, this combination sets up a vicious cycle in which the more depressed you feel, the more you drink, which in turn leads to more depression.

Insomnia

All of us occasionally have problems falling asleep. However, when a person misses several nights of restful sleep, he or she begins to feel out of sync with the rest of his or her life. Given enough time, the brain and the body will begin to manifest depressive symptoms.

Case Study #8 - The Sleepy Teen

Years ago, I was working in a church as a youth pastor. A friend of mine, who was a pharmacist, called me one day and indicated that he really needed to get his son in to see me. He feared his son had become psychotic because he was acting really weird. When I saw the young man, he looked pretty rough. He was disheveled, his eyes were swollen, he didn't look like he was really in the game, so to speak, and after about twenty minutes it became evident that something serious was going on.

This young man, who was about sixteen, had lost his first love. They had been together for six or seven months when he discovered that she had cheated on him. She was dating another guy. So, as we talked about this and how it made him feel, he told me he'd been thinking about it so much that he had not slept a single night through for nearly a week.

44

Research tells us that most of us can go maybe four days with the minimum amount of sleep, and then if we get a chance to rest up, we reset our sleep clock. In this case, this boy had not been able to do that. He had slept maybe ten hours in the past five days. If you don't get enough sleep, you feel depressed. He was even to the point of hallucinating and hearing voices.

I suggested he and his dad talk to his family physician and discussed getting him some short-term sleep aids. They put him on sleep medication for five days. I saw the young man in church about ten days later. He looked completely renewed and refreshed, and he told me he was sleeping well. He also said the hallucinations were gone and that he wasn't feeling suicidal. So sometimes simply getting your normal sleeping pattern reestablished helps you feel better.

Chronic Illness

For a countless number of people, chronic illness and depression are brutal facts of life. A chronic illness is a condition that lasts a long time and usually cannot be cured completely, although some of these illnesses can be controlled with diet, exercise, and certain medications. Examples of chronic illness include diabetes, heart disease, arthritis, kidney disease, HIV/AIDS, lupus, and multiple sclerosis.

People with chronic illness may experience depression. In fact, depression is one of the most common complications of chronic illness. It is estimated that up to one-third of individuals with a serious medical condition experience depression.[20]

Serious illness causes frightening changes in a person's lifestyle, personality, and relationships. Illness limits an individual's mobility and independence and makes it impossible to participate in enjoyable activities. Illness undercuts self-confidence and steals hope. Therefore, it is not surprising that people with chronic illness often experience a certain level of despair and sadness.

In many cases, the medications a person takes for his or her illness may also lead to more depression. WebMD.com[21] maintains an exhaustive list of medications that may cause changes in the way we feel.

Case Study #9 - The Receptionist

Frieda had been working at Dr. Barry Mead's office for more than twenty-three years. She was the doctor's first, and only, receptionist. Dr. Mead and his wife, Mary, had been impressed with Frieda's friendliness, attention to detail, and her way with people ever since they had met her nearly twenty-five years ago. She had become a vital part of their team since opening the practice, but Dr. Mead began to notice some changes in her.

She seemed more depressed, isolated, and grumpy. He also noted that she seemed to be drinking more fluids and going to the bathroom frequently. The clincher came when he asked about her weight loss. "Frieda, are you losing weight?"

Frieda's brow furrowed. "Yes, but I'm not really trying to. I must have a bug or something."

Dr. Mead caught up with her before locking up the office at the end of the day and asked if she would consider getting a blood test in the next couple of days. She agreed and within a couple of days the results were in. Dr. Mead invited her into this office to tell her she was a diabetic, and probably had been for the past year or two.

Though it took her by surprise, since she was only a few pounds overweight, she was curious to know more. Dr. Mead referred her to a diabetes educator, got her on some appropriate medications, and Frieda is now feeling much better. Knowledge is power. Now Frieda monitors her blood sugar, eats better, exercises, and gets proper rest. She is also more productive, and her pleasant disposition has returned. She knows she will have to be diligent to manage her diabetes, but she also feels support from her family, friends, and co-workers.

Millions of Americans are either pre-diabetics or are undiagnosed diabetics. Take a few minutes to get tested—especially if your family has a history of the disease.

The Depression-Prone Personality

Studies in the field of personality over the last quarter of a century show that most personality traits are highly heritable.[22] The depression-prone person may have inherited a strong predisposition to sadness or anxiety. While these findings may discourage some people, the truth is that a person can learn to feel better, learn to turn down the volume of the negativity, and have a happier life.

A depressed person has a pronounced tendency to think about things from a negative perspective. For example, when a person becomes depressed, it is much easier to decide what is wrong about a relationship, rather than what is right. Or a depressed person does not focus on what good can come from a task, but rather speaks pointedly about why the task is tedious or boring. When an individual allows negative thinking to run rampant, depression easily arises. Negative thinking is both a root cause of depression and a perpetuator of the problem.

Even though a person is currently caught in a negative thinking pattern, he or she may not always have had such tendencies. Over the years in my practice I have heard clients say, "I haven't always been this way. I used to be much more optimistic about things." However, whether the negative thinking is only temporary or is a deeply-ingrained habit, it is like poison to our emotions. The solution is not to sugarcoat every situation in life. Balance is necessary.

Case Study #10 - The Engineer

Sam had been working as a software engineer contractor in the Colorado Springs area for fifteen years. Shelby, his wife of seventeen years, confronted him about his long-standing negativity. She had finally had enough of his black-and-white thinking. Before all of this started, she remembered him being cool and calculating, but since their kids hit their teen years, Sam's negativity and sadness had become more pronounced. He always sounded as if he saw the glass half empty. He seemed to have decision constipation about everything he did. His constant negative ruminating had nearly pushed Shelby to seek a divorce.

Sam and Shelby decided to attend a "Get a Grip on Depression" class I conducted at the Navigator's International Headquarters near Colorado Springs. While attending, they began to understand that one piece of the puzzle for Sam was his basic thinking style. Sam has what

4. The fourth element is creating a trauma narrative. This narrative includes the losses and gains, the grief and the gratitude, as well as the vulnerability and strength that were experienced and called upon during the trauma.

5. The fifth element consists the overarching life principles and life lessons being learned.

Case Study #11 - The Earthquake

I met Claire several years ago while doing some consulting work at a local psychiatric hospital. She'd been admitted to the adult unit because she was suicidal. As we began our session, she told me how she had recently moved from the San Francisco area to Albuquerque, New Mexico, because she was tired of living in an earthquake zone. Four months earlier, she'd been sitting on her sofa watching the World Series when she heard a low rumble and looked out of the window to see that her building was swaying, at the same time ABC sports anchors were reporting an earthquake at Candlestick Park.

Before the earthquake hit, she had difficulty sleeping because her apartment bedroom was next to the elevator. After the earthquake, the vibrations from the elevator caused her to awake in a panic and filled her with anxiety. The accumulation of stress from the earthquake, the loss of sleep, and moving to a new area had overwhelmed her brain, body, and spirit.

Over the next several days the psychiatrist at the hospital was able to find the right medications to help her brain settle down. Group therapy, art therapy, individual counseling, and a good treatment plan helped her begin to rebuild her life. The social worker talked with the apartment management company, which allowed Claire to move. Several months later, I spoke with her outpatient therapist, who reported that Claire had a good job, had joined a local church, and was doing much better.

Anger/Resentment

The emotions of anger and resentment evolve from how a person manages emotional and physical pain. Scripture addresses bitterness and resentment and tells us to process anger appropriately. In Ephesians 4:26-

27 (NASB), the apostle Paul says we can be angry: "Be angry, and yet do not sin; do not let the sun go down on your anger, and do not give the devil an opportunity." There is an appointed time to be angry, and that's particularly true if it's righteous anger.

I don't know about you, but when someone cuts me off in traffic, the first thought in my head is not, "Hallelujah! Thank you, Jesus." If I had the power to condemn that car and driver to a very bad place, I might. However, typically within a couple of seconds, I realize I have probably cut people off in traffic, too, so I refuse to allow my anger to expand; I try to thank the Lord that we are both okay and continue on with my day.

In my counseling office, I see people who get upset and offended, and rather than dealing with the wound directly, they wallow in the hurt because they replay the offense over and over. Growing up in the South, my momma did a great job in raising me. One of her pearls of wisdom was to tell me not to pick at my scabs. But I, like most boys between eight and twelve years old, did pick at my scabs. I know it's gross, and I know right now some of you are saying, "Ewww," but stay with me for a minute. Momma would say, "If you keep picking it, it won't heal. And if you keep picking at it, you're going to leave a big ol ugly scar there." This principle applies to emotional wounds as well.

Unfortunately, some mental health professionals make a living helping people find a way to rehearse their hurts by picking their scabs. Sometimes in therapy we need to go back and look at those hurts and try to get a different perspective on them. It's important to do, and I do it from time to time with my clients. However, therapists and clients need to be careful about continually rehearsing the hurts.

The Bible speaks to this in Hebrews 12:15 (NIV): "See to it that no one falls short of the grace of God and that no bitter root grows up to cause trouble and defile many." If you hold on to anger and resentment, if you fail to process it, if you fail to move to a place where you can forgive, then you risk never having the ability to manage your depression.

Medications

Medications that are prescribed for various medical conditions can cause feelings of sadness, hopelessness, despair, and discouragement. Other medications make you feel excessive joy, or in some cases, mania.

Medications that cause mania or depression appear to alter brain chemicals in some way. And even though the drugs may be necessary to treat the condition, the side effect is hardly acceptable. As an example, Accutane™, which is prescribed for the treatment of acne, has been found to also cause depression. So have oral contraceptives, high blood pressure drugs, and even statins that treat high cholesterol.

The best way to avoid drugs that affect your mood is to know which medicines commonly cause depression and/or mania. Then talk to your doctor to see if it's possible to try another medication. Your doctor should let you know up front which drugs might cause feelings of depression or mania. WebMD.com maintains one of the most current lists available. [25] Local pharmacists are also able to help with this information.

Larger Societal/ Cultural Issues

The National Institute for Mental Health's research shows that larger societal and cultural concerns like political unrest, economic factors, modernization and industrialization, high divorce rates, and poverty may also be contributing to the higher rates of depression. The actual verbalization of depression—the way people talk about depression—in terms of specific symptoms is also affected by cultural factors.[26]

In a study of more than 200 participants, half from an outpatient clinic in China and half from a clinical research department in the United States, researchers found out some surprising results.

Overall, the data showed a greater level of psychological symptoms reporting in the North American sample.

East Asian participants reported a significantly higher level of somatic symptoms.[27]

Relationships

Relationships negatively or positively influence depression. For example, negative events in a relationship like conflict, breaking up, or discovering that your partner is having an affair can make a person's depression worse, even pushing him or her toward suicidal thoughts. Likewise, pressures at work, a breach of trust between friends, or a family feud are additional examples of relationship stressors that lead to negative feelings and increase a person's feelings of sadness and depression.

Steve and Brenda had been dating about six months after meeting on a Christian online dating service. It started off slow, with emailing, shared photos, and a couple of brief videos. After meeting in public for the first time, they both felt safe and began to slowly develop their relationship. They were cautiously excited about the relationship as they spent more time with one another. Steve thought he'd kept the pace slow, only kissing Brenda after the fourth date.

Steve thought that things were fine when he received a text from Brenda. The note said, "Steve, you are a really nice guy, but I am not ready for this relationship. I think we need to call it off." Steve was devastated; it was the first serious relationship he'd been in for quite some time.

As he drove home from work that evening he was filled with doubt about his abilities as a man to have and hold onto relationships. He had received texts, emails, and phone messages like this in other relationships. The thoughts began to creep into his head, "Steve, let's face it, no woman wants to be with you; you are such a loser." Steve's brain was rolling all manner of negative thoughts around, much like sagebrush rolling across the desert in New Mexico. He could feel some of the old familiar thoughts of worthlessness, and when they begin to point him in the direction of ending it all, he realized that he'd let things go way too far.

He remembered that some of his "man friends" were having a meal and Bible study that evening. He quickly turned right and showed up at Cracker Barrel and joined in. He never felt like he needed to go into the details of what had happened earlier that evening. Instead, he leaned into the Bible study material, which was on Philippians 4:8 and managing your thought life. As the meeting broke up that night, Steve was silently and prayerfully relieved that he'd chosen to spend time with his friends.

Over the next several weeks Steve and Brenda were able to reconnect and are moving forward with their relationship.

Example of Grief and Loss

Depression involves intense emotions that we would prefer not to experience. However, depression is a normal part of resolving a loss. As we begin to realize what we have lost, we will experience painful emotions. These reactions are part of the hard work of becoming aware of the significance of the loss. This tough but necessary work can be thought of as "grief work." Grief work involves identifying our losses by experiencing the strong emotions that accompany the losses before we can let them go.

Loss also leads to depression. Dr. Archibald Hart has written on this subject extensively.[28] He indicates that we go through four types of losses, and most of the research indicates that depression is usually tied to some type of loss. Those losses can be broken down into four areas.

1. **Concrete loss.** If you can remember the time and date of a certain loss, then you have experienced a concrete loss. This could be the anniversary of the death of a family member or the date a family pet died. The first loss I can remember was a family dog in 1957 or '58. The dog's name was Yeller, and we had had him for a while. One day he ran out in front of a car. We couldn't do anything for him, so my dad had to put him down.

   It's a good thing for a son to see his father model compassion and empathy the way my dad did that day. I still remember, even though I am in my sixties. It hasn't really impacted me in a negative way because I processed the loss appropriately.

   I have been working in one capacity or another most of my life, and along the way I've have been through two downsizings in the workplace. Job loss is a concrete loss as well. In our recent economic downturn, many have experienced this type of loss or at least know someone who has.

2. **Abstract loss.** Abstract loss is usually related to a concrete loss. It is abstract because it is not something you can touch or about which you can remember specific details. You can feel it, but you can't touch it. When I hear someone talk about losing a pet, I remember the pain I felt when I lost Yeller. This loss is described in a more abstract way—it's a feeling, it's a thought, it's an impression, and it's part of a normal process of grieving.

3. **Imagined loss.** Imagined loss is all of those "what ifs" and "only ifs." If only I had done this. If only I had done that. If only this had happened. If only this hadn't happened. This type of loss is difficult to deal with because you really can't do anything about it. It's a time stealer, it is a time bandit; it will absorb more and more of your mind with little resolution. You can't grieve imagined loss.

4. **Threatened loss.** The "what if" question also steals time and space in our brain. It is a loss that may or may not happen. (For example, a man feels a lump on his neck; his doctor performs a biopsy, but the results are not in.)

We'll go into more depth about each of the types of loss in the next chapter, but I want to introduce these to you right now because more often than not, depression is usually related to a loss or combination of losses or series of losses in a person's life.

Here are some additional causes of depression.

Loneliness

Loneliness has a couple of unique definitions. Some see loneliness as being without company, cut off from others. Others see loneliness as sadness from being alone. Unrelenting loneliness can push a person into depression if it leads him or her to become desolate and withdrawn from fellowship.

Brain, Mind, Body Issues

Traumatic brain injury (TBI), addictions, and other forms of head injuries can severely impair an individual and increase the incidents of depression, anxiety, and impulse control issues. When the brain is healthy and the mind is thinking the right types of thoughts, your brain is able to process joy, happiness, sadness, elation, and love. If the brain gets damaged, then it doesn't work properly. It's like your computer when it is bogged down with a virus.

Case Study #12 - The Soldier

Jason joined his local Army National Guard unit before graduating from high school in May 2001. He was looking forward to serving in the Guard as his father, grandfather, and uncle had done. His grandfather's unit had been mobilized for WWII. His uncle had been mobilized in Little Rock during the Little Rock Central High School Integration Crisis in 1957 and 1958. His dad was active during the Cold War. All had served with honor.

Jason was excited to follow his family's tradition of service. He planned to start college the winter after he finished basic training and advanced individual training at Fort Benning, Georgia. Jason would be a part-time soldier and student. Then 9/11 happened. Over the next couple of years, he and thousands of other reserve and active duty soldiers waited for orders.

In 2003, the order was issued and his unit was placed into federal service. In 2004, they were deployed to Iraq where Jason was "in country" (in the combat zone). Within a few months he was awarded the Combat Infantryman's Badge as a result of serving with his unit. During his year of deployment, Jason was involved in one fire fight and got blown up (a term used for being hit by an improvised explosive device, an IED) three times.

Within a few months of returning home and returning to school, he starting experiencing headaches, and a darkness began to creep up on him. He had a hard time staying focused and began to pull away from others. A few months later, an Army psychologist came by during his unit's monthly drill and gave a talk on traumatic brain injury. Jason and several of his buddies who had been "blown up" in Iraq talked with the doctor about what had happened to them.

Over the next several months Jason became involved in a TBI research study for soldiers and showed steady improvement. His schoolwork improved, he began to re-engage with family and friends, and continued to serve in the Guard. In 2007, he returned with his unit for his second tour and came home without any injuries.

Since then, Jason has finished his enlistment with the Guard, has gotten married, and is considering pursuing a master's degree. He still has some challenging days in front of him, but he has been able to manage and work with his TBI issues.

Studies done on fellow veterans—particularly from the Iraq and Afghanistan wars—as well as studies on athletes continue to shed light and valuable information concerning the brain and the mind-body connection.

A person's mind is like a computer. In this analogy, the mind is the operating system. If a person has a healthy brain and a healthy outlook on life, then he or she will be able to interpret life's experiences in a way that's appropriate. A healthy brain and a healthy mind help push back depression.

However, if an individual has a pessimistic thinking style—if he or she tends to see the glass as half empty, or tends to see things like Eeyore from Winnie-the-Pooh, in a negative frame of mind—then the result will be unhappy thoughts, feelings, and behaviors. If your belief system is pessimistic, then you're going to have a more negative outcome. If you have more of an optimistic outlook, then you'll have more positive outcomes.

Trigger Events

Here is a list of situations that can cascade into depression or depressive reactions:

❖ Rejection

❖ Failure

❖ Insults

❖ Being victimized

❖ Loss

❖ Cumulative life stress

❖ Lack of positive, rewarding life events

❖ A reaction to success (depression can occur after a particular experience of success or achievement that may have been stressful)

❖ Learned helplessness

God-sent Trials

St. John of the Cross (1542-1591), a Catholic mystic writer in the 16th century, wrote a book titled *The Dark Night of the Soul.* He said our spiritual walk sometimes includes times in which we feel absent from God's presence. The lesson he learned through prayer, reflection, and study is that sometimes this feeling of God's absence happens because God wants us to grow up, spiritually and emotionally. When we go through that dark night of the soul, it may not be caused by clinical depression, bad thinking, or a lack of sleep. God might be trying to get our attention. Such God-sent trials are meant to prune or purify us so we bear more fruit. As someone put it, God tries to bring forth the good in us, whereas Satan tempts us to bring forth the evil, or the worst, in us.

The dark night is not something bad or destructive. God's purpose for the darkness is not to punish or afflict us; it is to set us free. Darkness is one of the ways in which God brings us to a hush—a stillness—so He can work transformation in our soul. When you recognize the dark night for what it is, you can be grateful that God is lovingly drawing you away from every distraction so you can see Him.

If you are going through this right now, don't be disheartened. I've been a believer for more than forty years and I've been through that dark place a few times. I know it isn't any fun. The good news, as Scripture says, is, "He who began a good work in you will be faithful to complete it" (Philippians 1:6 NIV). So even on those dark days when you feel like you are at the end of your rope, make a knot and hang on because it could be a God-sent trial. When you get through it, God has some great things planned for you. Until then, trust Him, and get around people who will encourage you. Trust that God will show you His plan and purpose.

Case Study #13 – The Customer Service Representative

One of my clients recently told me he was coming out of a long, dry wintertime in his life. Within an eight-month period, he and his wife had both lost jobs and their son had begun abusing prescription medication. This dark, cold season had been a difficult, painful time in which the love of God seemed far away.

He learned that these trials were God-sent and that they were designed to prune and purify (John 15:2, 1 Peter 1:6-7) in order for him to bear more fruit. After a three-week pity party he decided to go to worship services with his wife. He said, "It was like God had a special message for me that morning. The pastor was preaching from Romans 8, and when he was reading the passage about how 'nothing can separate us from the love of God,' it hit me. God knows exactly what I am going through." Soon he connected with some other men through a men's small group at his church.

Through these key relationships with men, he believed he could "man up" as a believer and begin to fearlessly trust God to provide for him and his family.

As he and his wife began to put their lives back together, and as he learned to trust the Lord, he felt a peace in his soul and a new purpose in his life. In a few months, he was working and feeling more productive. He and his wife are actively involved in the small group ministry of their church, and they recently returned from a mission trip to Guatemala.

Sin, Bitterness

Sometimes depression is a direct consequence of sin, but this does not mean that all depression is the result of personal sin. Some examples of a sin-based depression might include attitudes like resentment, bitterness, being unwilling to forgive; or behaviors such as willful disobedience, expressing sexuality outside the confines of marriage, and living in fear of the future.

If you run around outside in the wintertime in bad weather without the proper protection, you increase the likelihood that you'll get sick. If you don't get enough sleep and don't take care of yourself, you increase the risk that you're going to get sick. If you violate the laws of nature long enough, they're going to bite you eventually. If you choose to drive fast on the interstate—and I've done this, so I'm a fellow struggler—then you do so with the knowledge that you might get caught, and if you are, you will have to face the consequences.

If you get popped for speeding, thank the officer and get with the program because you violated the laws of the land, which is a sin. So if you've gotten caught up in an addiction or a bad habit and consequently are feeling like you're trapped, I encourage you to deal with it. If you need to talk to a pastor or a priest for help, then do that. All of us sin. All of us struggle. Sometimes we need a little help to overcome our sin and struggles. 1 John 1:8-9 (NLT) says, "If we claim we have no sin, we are only fooling ourselves and not living in the truth. But if we confess our sins to him, he is faithful and just to forgive us our sins and cleanse us from all wickedness."

Irrational, Unbiblical Self-talk, or Misbeliefs

The field of positive psychology (the psychological study of what makes life most worth living) helps us understand that typical depression triggers are not what make us feel depressed as much as our mental attitude or interpretation of the trigger event.

So what are some other causes of depression? One cause could be irrational, unbiblical thinking. Sometimes those thoughts are the messages we got as children growing up. If you had a parent who was controlling and he or she told you that you would never measure up, or that you wouldn't do this or you couldn't do that, then you grew up believing what you were told. We often file the flight plan that other people give us. If my parents had told me I'd never finish school, odds are I wouldn't have.

When I was in the tenth grade, I had an English teacher who told me on multiple occasions that she doubted I would ever make it through high school because I didn't know "diddly squat" about writing. When a strong woman tells a tenth grade boy something like that, the message

60

gets into your head and it hangs around. For years, any time I wrote something, I could hear her voice in my head.

I still introduce myself in writers groups by saying, "Hi, I'm John, and I'm a grammatically challenged writer." They all laugh, but the truth is, I was a horrible grammar student, at least according to my teacher.

Ten years ago, I was at a writers conference and I told a friend what my teacher said and how I still hear her voice when I write.

"You're a great writer," my friend said. "You aren't great with grammar, but there are several of us here who love grammar and we would love to help. So why don't you focus on writing your ideas and stories and let us help you with your grammar."

I wish I had figured this out sooner. Instead, I allowed a teacher to put a flight plan in my head that said I would never be a writer, and her words paralyzed my writing attempts for decades.

When I received my first and second master's degrees, I wanted to make a copy of my diplomas and mail them to that teacher, but I decided not to. The first piece of writing I ever got paid for was an assignment from Focus on the Family. I think it was titled *Horrormones and Your Adolescents. Is it Depression or is it Just Horrormones?* When I received the check for the article, I was so proud. It was the first time I'd ever been paid to write anything. My friends did help me with the grammar. It was real affirming for me to say, "Yes, I have been paid to write. I'm a professional writer."

Now I write for Sage magazine, and I write articles for my website, and I even do a little blogging. I am still grammatically challenged, but I write anyway. So if you've got some irrational, unbiblical thinking stuck in your head, the next two or three sections will give you some practical tools to help you learn to push back on that type of thinking.

True Guilt vs. Shame or False Guilt

Guilt is another possible cause of depression. For example, King David stated, "When I kept silent about my sin, my body wasted away through my groaning all day long" (Psalm 32:3 NASB). Guilt is a feeling that can be experienced as a sin against God or man. The apostle Paul said, "And herein do I exercise myself, to have always a conscience void of offence toward God, and toward men" (Acts 24:16 KJV).

If the sin is against God, the solution is quite straightforward. The solution is found in 1 John 1:9 (KJV), "If we confess [agree with God about] our sins, he is faithful and just to forgive us our sins, and to cleanse us from all unrighteousness." Once an individual asks God to forgive him or her for a sin, God grants forgiveness and remembers it no more. Unfortunately, the individual may still feel guilty if he or she has not firmly grasped the mercy of God, but this type of guilt is not of God.

Some sins also affect other people, and although God forgives the sin completely, an obligation still exists toward the offended person. The love of Christ directs us to seek forgiveness, if possible, from those we have offended. In twelve-step programs, the "making amends" to those we have injured or offended is a major point in the road to healing. Certainly going to another individual and asking for forgiveness is not always possible, or even appropriate, but when it is, it is a major positive force in assuaging true guilt.

False guilt arises from a sense of personal shortcoming and is usually shame-based. Obsessive-compulsive personality types are particularly prone to this kind of false guilt because this personality type tends to be characterized by being excessively rigid, conscientious, and perfectionistic. Such individuals may be absorbed in right and wrong, or exhibit excessively dutiful traits, and are unable to be spontaneous or liberated. Their conscience will not allow it. False guilt usually arises out of a sense of being permanently flawed, unacceptable, and unlovable. People dealing with a great deal of false guilt may make repeated confessions of "sin" to God and repeated apologies to others for perceived offenses, but these turn out to be equally unproductive in alleviating their ongoing oppressive sense of guilt. People suffering from false guilt usually need professional counseling to help dissect the underlying patterns of self-critical thought and the roots of damage to their self-esteem that fuel the constant flow of false guilt through their personality.

The Biochemical "Three-legged Stool"

This three-legged stool paradigm is a rudimentary way to illustrate a complex interplay between the brain's neurotransmitters, thyroid hormone function, and gonadotropins (sexual hormones) within the body. A combination of one or more imbalances in these three major categories of hormones has a highly disruptive effect on the brain's capacity to maintain normalcy and results in the formation of symptoms of major depression. Individuals who are experiencing disruptions in the balance of neurotransmitters (for example, serotonin, norepinephrine, or dopamine) are in need of biological intervention with appropriate medication and may be suffering from a brain illness.

While depression is perpetuated by intrapersonal struggles, sometimes biochemical difficulties add to the problem. Our bodies have neurotransmitters (such as serotonin and norepinephrine) that help regulate emotional and mental stability. If these transmitters are out of balance, the brain may not be able to properly maintain stability. When this occurs, the medical profession refers to this type of depression as biochemical.

In addition, medications prescribed by physicians for other physical problems (high blood pressure, for example) may cause depression. Consumption of alcohol or recreational drugs increases a person's tendency toward depression. In light of these physical possibilities, it is wise for a person who has significantly deep and lasting struggles with depression to be thoroughly examined by a competent physician or psychiatrist.

Case Study #14 - Medication Change

Jennie's doctor had recently changed her medication for hyperthyroidism when she came to my office. Her pastor had noticed she was more down and depressed. One Sunday she was praying at the altar when the pastor's wife approached her and asked to pray with her. The pastor's wife called her husband over, and after a time of prayer and godly counsel, they suggested that Jennie call my office. Her pastor had been trained in spiritual first aid and was a seasoned professional when it came to helping people in crisis. He and his wife provided solid, biblical, and appropriate counseling and comfort to Jennie.

When I shook her hand, I noted how cool it was. As we reviewed her medical and family history, she mentioned the change in medication and the change in her mood. With her permission, I contacted her physician, who concurred that the medication adjustment could be the cause of her depression. We both agreed to watch her for the next several weeks.

Within the next nine weeks the medicine helped to stabilize her hyperthyroidism and Jennie no longer felt depressed. I will never forget our last session. When I shook her hand, it was as warm as toast. Jennie reports feeling great and is doing well with diet, the adjustment in her medication, and a positive attitude. She also shared that her relationship with the Lord was growing.

When your medication types or dosages change, it is wise to observe your mood and attitude levels. You may stabilize in a few weeks as did Jennie, but if the symptoms persist, be sure to talk to your physician about changing or adjusting your medication. It might also help to check in with your spouse or friends to see if they notice any changes. It is important that you and your prescriber communicate about any changes in your mood or thinking processes.

Genetic Factors in Affective (Depressive) Illness

The medical community is still a long way from fully understanding the biology of mood disorders, but it has become the target of converging lines of investigation that are consistently yielding new discoveries. Researchers are learning about the structure and functioning of the brain in people with mood disorders, the role of chemical neurotransmitters and the endocrine system, the influence of sleep, and other psychological cycles. Based on studies mentioned earlier, there is a relationship between your genetic makeup and a susceptibility to depression.

Dysfunctional or Unworkable Priorities

Priorities become dysfunctional or unworkable when a person reaches a position in life that is not satisfactory. He feels like his priorities are out of balance and his objectives are clouded or she questions her personal significance. Questions such as, "What am I giving my life to?" and "Is there any purpose in my existence?" weigh heavily on the individual.

Distorted priorities affect an individual's relationship with God, with his family, and with himself. These personal relationships are overlooked and brushed aside for the more urgent and tyrannical demands of our environment. A chronic diet of overwork, unrealistic priorities, and a growing sense of futility and purposelessness become significant contributing factors to a major depressive disorder, especially in the mid to later years of life.

God is clear when He tells us what it takes to have a life of fulfillment. For example, He tells us to love Him with our entire being (Matthew 22:37); He encourages us to share His love with those with whom we come in contact (1 John); to give priority to our family (1 Timothy 5:8); and to connect to a Bible-believing, New Testament church (1 Timothy 3:15). God has outlined a plan for our lives that, if faithfully followed, brings us the joy we desire.

People, particularly Christians, who fall into a period of depression usually admit they have gone counter to the priorities God has given us in the Bible. I have often spoken with depressed Christians who admit they have not done all they know to do in following God's will for their lives. For example, a depressed businessperson may admit he has placed his career ahead of his spiritual or family needs. Or perhaps a man knows the Scripture's instruction to have a temperate, kind nature has given in to tendencies of extreme competitiveness. A depressed woman may have allowed a finicky nature to displace her usually gentle spirit. Although depressed people know what is biblically right, in spite of their knowledge, they often blindly pursue other matters.

If we view depression as being caused in part by inappropriate priorities, then we may presume that God allows depression so we will recognize our need to put our lives in proper order.

Depression is like a snowball, though. A person who is depressed becomes depressed further about being depressed. Self-condemnation, worrying about our spiritual well-being, feeling rejected by God, and fearing that friends will not understand are all complicating issues that further decrease our hope and therefore increase our depression.

Spiritual Warfare

Another thing that impacts depression is spiritual warfare. There's more going on in our world than what we see. There is an enemy who doesn't like us. We should not be afraid of him because he is a created being. Spiritual warfare is part of the Christian life.

I believe the main way the enemy attacks us is through our thoughts, and if he deceives us, he wins. He tries to get us to believe we are worthless, that we'll never measure up, and when we embrace those lies, we are paralyzed spiritually. However, the book of Revelation (12:10-11) identifies him as an accuser. He accuses believers 24/7. So let me ask you this: What does an accuser do? He puts you down. He tries to fill you with doubt and confusion. And he tries to cause you to stumble in your walk with Christ.

Yet the passage in Revelation says, "They overcame him because of the blood of the Lamb and because of the word of their testimony." Our job is to learn what Scripture says about us, who we are in Christ, and what God wants to do for and in us. And yet we tend to listen to other voices—including the negative feedback Satan plants in our minds. Spiritual warfare ties into spiritual armor.

In Ephesians 6:10-20, the apostle Paul tells us that we take our stand against Satan's schemes by standing firm with the belt of truth, the breastplate of righteousness, and with feet fitted with the readiness that comes from the gospel of peace. He also tells us to take up the shield of faith, to put on the helmet of salvation and the sword of the Spirit (the Word of God).

Spiritual warfare has an impact on how we think, act, and feel. As we come to an end of this section about the causes of depression, meditate on Scripture.

"For as he thinks in his heart, so is he" (Proverbs 23:7 AMP).

We are a byproduct of our thought life. If we think good thoughts, positive thoughts, happy thoughts, guess what we feel? Good, positive, and happy. If we tend to have more of a pessimistic mindset, we will see the glass as half empty, we will see the days as gray, and we will tend to be more like Eeyore. How we think will determine how we feel.

"Fix your thoughts on what is true and pure and lovely and admirable. Think about things that are excellent and worthy of praise" (Philippians 4:8 NLT).

For years I've been sharing this truth with my clients: "Nothing stays in your head rent free." Did you get that? Nothing stays in your head rent free. Take some time to review these contributors or causes of depression. Look deep within and see if some of these negative issues and painful events have led to you being stuck. And if you're feeling like God has abandoned you or that you never had a relationship with Him, then pray. "Lord, I'm feeling really stuck and I need to feel Your presence. I need You to speak to me. I need You to love me."

When you pray a prayer like that, expect to hear from the Lord. If you need to confess a sin, do so. And then be accountable to other growing believers. In the following chapters you are going to learn how to change your thought life, how to understand the losses you have experienced, how to break free from bondage by thinking correctly. Victory over your struggles is possible.

Depression involves intense emotions that we would prefer not to experience. The fact is, however, that depression is a normal part of resolving a loss. As we begin to realize what we have lost, we will experience painful emotions. These are part of the hard work of becoming aware of the significance of the loss. This hard but necessary work is called "grief work." Grief work involves identifying our losses by experiencing the strong emotions that accompany the losses before we let them go.

"For as he thinks in his heart, so is he."

Proverbs 23:7 (AMP)

Chapter 3

Learning Your ATCs

Depressed people come to pastors and counselors because they are puzzled and sometimes frightened about their feelings of sadness, despair, and depression. "I wish I could understand my emotions," some say. Others ask, "If I don't like my emotions, how can I change them?"

The first thing to learn about understanding our feelings or emotions is that we cannot control them directly, but they are side effects of something we directly command—our thoughts. For the sake of clarity, let's consider feelings and emotions as the same thing. The thinking process that causes our emotions involves our beliefs, which we internally recite to ourselves—"self-talk." Feelings cannot be classified as good or bad because feelings are only signals of our present self-talk. Emotions are like a smoke alarm, faithfully responding to the stimuli of the beliefs we are using as we evaluate each circumstance.

What we believe is partially determined by the programming we absorb from our early childhood to the present. Our parents, siblings, peers, teachers, faith groups, significant others, books, TV, and so on, all contribute to our perceptions about the world and ourselves. As mentioned in the introduction, there are two basic mindsets people deal with: the "fixed mindset" and the "growth mindset."

If a person is in a fixed mindset and something bad or negative occurs, the following things happen. He or she tends to think:

69

❖ It's personal (it's all my fault)

❖ It's permanent (it cannot be changed)

❖ It's pervasive (it will affect everything)

Before I show you a few tools to change the way you think, let's consider how the fixed mindset works in our minds.

To deal with the negativity of a fixed mindset, we must learn our ATCs—activating event, thought, and consequences. In the true examples below, you will see how ATC works together in a natural fashion.

An activating event is a trigger—a challenge, an adversity, or a positive event—and it comes automatically, based on your belief system. Your thoughts are the interpretation of the activating event, which shows up in your self-talk. It's what you say to yourself in the heat of the moment after the trigger event has occurred. The consequence is a combination of what you feel and the behavioral response tied to those feelings. With each thought, you have an immediate consequence. Every event is followed by a sequence of thoughts and behaviors.

If you decide to purchase a new dress or buy a new tool, that decision is the trigger. In this case, the trigger is a positive event; you are excited about your purchase. However, a trigger can be good, bad, or neutral. It depends on what you do with it.

Advertisers spend billions of dollars a year to either remind you of a special memory or create a new one to provide you an opportunity to purchase their product.

Fiction writers call this the inciting incident—it's the moment in the novel when the protagonist's normal world gets turned upside down and we, as the readers, get to see how he or she will react.

A positive example of a trigger might include a random craving for freshly baked cookies. Your mind immediately begins to consider where you might find some—the nearest bakery, your aunt, or your mother, to name a few.

70

A negative example of a trigger would be to hand a store clerk your credit card for a purchase. She runs the card and says, "I'm sorry. It's been declined." What do you say to yourself in that moment?

At that point the negative thoughts probably cascade through your mind as you attempt to deal with the flood of thoughts and feelings. Because you feel embarrassed you might feel like saying, "It can't be maxed out. There's no way." Or you might say, "This clerk must think I am a complete idiot." Or you might wonder, "What did my husband or wife buy that I didn't know about?" You feel the heat of embarrassment on your face for a few seconds, catch your breath, and pull out another card to successfully complete the transaction. As you head to the parking lot you recall that your wife had to take your five-year-old to urgent care and you are grateful that you had the additional card with you.

The key question to ask yourself when a negative trigger occurs is, "Is my reaction to the activating event helping or harming, appropriate or inappropriate?" As you learn to challenge old misbeliefs, you will experience more success in pushing back angry thoughts, anxious thoughts, unedifying thoughts, or depressive thoughts.

The Bible says, "As a man thinketh, so is he" (Proverbs 23:7 KJV). Part of what we want to do with this ATC training is to help you understand how to identify those thought processes and change them into a more biblical process.

After we trust Christ for salvation, we are illuminated by the Holy Spirit to understand more and more of the Word of God, which sanctifies and transforms our behavior and feelings as we renew our minds on a regular basis. We thus learn to evaluate each circumstance with beliefs and self-talk, looking at the larger picture of God's purpose and love in everything. We call this "faith-oriented self-talk."

Negative emotions are often related to distorted thinking. We change our emotionally dysfunctional reactions to each circumstance by discovering our distorted misbeliefs, challenging them vigorously, and replacing our judgmental self-talk with truth- and faith-oriented self-talk.

Growing up in Fort Valley, Georgia, we knew two basic types of ants: black ants and red ants. The black ants showed up at picnics or in your house. They were a nuisance but didn't bite you. Red ants usually meant fire ants, and when they showed up, it was never a good outcome.

Red ants and automatic negative thoughts (ANT) are similar because they lead to negative outcomes. In identifying our automatic negative thoughts, or our stinking thinking, we need to be aware that no matter what the thought is, the sequence is always the same. An aggravating or positive event is quickly followed by an automatic thought process and a consequence that involves an emotional response and some type of behavior.

I want to go into detail here to help you understand how thoughts equal emotions and how these thought-emotions lead to reactions.

A movie; a story; an experience; a sight, sound, or smell;—especially if it reminds me of a loss—can be an activating event. A reduction in staff at my workplace—and me on the list to be downsized—is an activating event.

My emotional (thoughts) response to the event is sadness. Then I react by behaving in a certain way—perhaps withdrawal.

Do you see how the activating event is something that triggers a thought process about loss? The thought process is loss, the emotion is sadness, and the reaction or consequence is withdrawal.

Another trigger might be danger. Maybe you're in a new place. You're going to a new store, a new parking lot, or an unfamiliar part of town. Then your car breaks down. Your first thought is, "Oh my gosh, I'm in a dangerous place!" When you begin to think about the situation, if you believe you're in danger, the emotional reaction is always anxiety. That's the raw, exposed emotion you're feeling.

If you believe you are in danger, your emotions might be a combination of anxiety and uneasiness, and your behavior might become more aggressive or more passive. You might confront the danger, freeze in a panic, or call for help.

Suppose someone has violated your boundaries or someone at work puts you down or is talking about you. Maybe you hear something negative about yourself through a second or third party. The situation is your activating event.

The first emotion most people feel in an instance like this is anger. There are four ways people express anger.

The first type of anger is explosive anger. The person blows up making a lot of noise. It's intense. After the outburst, they feel better. Unfortunately, everybody around them feels deeply wounded because of the explosion.

The second type of anger is a passive/aggressive style of anger. The person stuffs his or her emotions for a while, and then suddenly blows up—sometimes at a later date over a much smaller issue.

The third type of anger is called somatized anger. In this case a person never allows a voice to his or her anger. Eventually, the anger shows up physically. It may appear as chronic gas, irritable bowel syndrome, headaches, or temporomandibular joint (TMJ). All these ailments may be induced by stress or internalized anger. This type of anger is like creamy smooth peanut butter on a Saltine cracker. If you press the cracker, the peanut butter seeps through the holes. That's what suppressing anger does.

The final type of anger is what I call passive-resistant anger. This type of anger occurs in a person who never seems to get angry but instead tends to get even. When I was a young lieutenant in the Army, we had to fill out travel paperwork in triplicate, with black ink only. Once, I inadvertently skipped a question that needed an A or B answer. When I turned in my paperwork, the young sergeant at the desk took my paperwork, read it over, then with a red magic marker put a big circle around my missed question. He said, "Sir, the form is not filled out correctly. You should have checked A or B."

In my mind, the simple solution would have been to simply point out my error. No big deal. But the sergeant made it a big deal, probably because of my lowly rank. He made me start over with a fresh form.

ATC applies to my situation.

What did I feel when he made me redo the form? I felt like he had violated a boundary with that big red circle on my paperwork. I thought he had trespassed against me. My emotional reaction was anger. I really couldn't show aggression there, but I would be lying to you if I told you I didn't have a few aggressive thoughts. In the end, he was technically right and I am glad I let it go. The sergeant and I developed a great relationship and worked well together on several projects over the next couple of years.

If you experience a negative aggravating event and that event causes you to think you're being violated or trespassed, typically the emotional reaction you're going to exhibit is anger, and the way you're going to act that out is some type of aggression.

At times, I have been short with my wife, Angie, and that has caused her harm. The harm wasn't physical, but that old saying that sticks and stones may break my bones but words will never harm me is a bunch of hooey. Hurting words hurt.

After I hurt her, my emotional reaction is guilt, and that's good. It's healthy guilt. When we hurt others, we ought to feel sorry for our actions or words. The emotional reaction, the guilt, should produce a behavioral response that shows us taking ownership for it, becoming accountable for our actions or words. It should lead to an apology, followed by a change in behavior.

The Bible talks about being quick to listen and slow to speak. A friend of mine, Dr. Jack Allen, a biblical ethicist, says, "If you've made a mess, own your mess, confess your mess, but then clean up your mess."

The next part of the process is we tend to compare ourselves to others in a negative way. We'll see someone we think is more handsome, smarter, makes more money, has a bigger car, or has a nicer house and the first thought we have is we can't measure up. We feel lower—less privileged, not as sharp, not as wealthy, not as cool, not as together. Negative comparison produces negative results.

When was the last time you gave into a negative comparison? What did you feel? Probably embarrassed, right? If you go someplace and you are overdressed or underdressed, your first thought process is a negative comparison. We want to become invisible when we are embarrassed. We want to blend into the background. I sure do.

But the opposite is also true. Think about a time in a small group, a team, a family setting, or even a work environment in which someone complimented you. Let's say you helped lead your team to accomplish a certain goal or task. Someone says, "Hey, you did a great job. We couldn't have succeeded without you." What's your first thought?

Wow! I made a positive contribution. Someone acknowledged the fact that I did something good.

Such thoughts produce pride—the appropriate kind (true pride shares the credit). You feel good about doing a job well. Having someone else acknowledge it makes you feel even better.

Looking at the ATC principles from a positive perspective, if the trigger event is something that (1) gives us insight and (2) understanding, and we get it, then we appreciate what we received. The emotional response is gratitude and the behavioral outcome is to give thanks.

A third positive outcome is settling into a normal routine. You realize how good your life is. I'm grateful to be an American. I'm grateful to live in a free enterprise system. I'm grateful to live in a country that allows me to determine my own future as long as my actions are legal, honorable, and ethical.

Our thoughts push us into reactions. Remember, an activating event can either be a negative or a positive. It leads to an automatic negative thought (ANT) or a positive thought. Everything you think leads to emotional reactions followed by a behavioral response.

Once we are heading in the right direction, we need to make sure we continue to do so without getting tripped up—a process psychology refers to as "cognitive distortions."

So what activities get us stuck? Why don't we experience a happier life? Why is it so difficult to break out of depression? Why do we get stuck in our stinking thinking? What can we do to become an ANT (automatic negative thoughts) eater, as Dr. Daniel Amen, psychiatrist and best-selling author, says?

ATC Practice Example

Activating event: You receive an email from your boss who wants to meet with you in his office before the end of the day.

Thoughts: What are some of your automatic, initial thoughts?

_____

_____

_____

_____

_____

Consequences: What are your feelings as you read the email?
What is your behavioral reaction to the email?
Is your reaction helpful or harmful? Please describe.

_____

_____

_____

_____

_____

_____

Chapter 4

The Stinking Thinking Traps

Stinking thinking corrupts your brain and triggers harmful mental states such as anxiety, anger, and depression. Unless you are willing to do some constructive re-engineering, your thinking becomes automatic, impulsive, and often wrong by bending, deleting, distorting, and exaggerating the truth. Your future is not defined by your past. Your thoughts can change, and consequently, your future can become totally different.

Let's begin with a description of how stinking thinking works so you will be able to push back the lies and replace them with truth.

For most of us, depression will be more about managing our thoughts, attitudes, and actions than about taking the right medications. In the exciting and growing field of positive psychology, advances are being made in the area of understanding how thinking influences our lives. Much of the positive psychology approach is consistent with what Christians believe, and since I am a Christ-follower, consistency is important to me.

Stinking thinking traps undermine mental toughness and performance and lead to an inaccurate understanding of the situation. Following are six common stinking thinking traps, or automatic negative thinking styles we have to identify and fight against. Use the critical questions included in these thinking traps to help you clarify your situation.

Jumping to Conclusions

The Bible contains a fascinating story about how jumping to conclusions causes trouble. To get the most out of it, be sure to read the whole story.

So the men of Reuben, Gad, and the half-tribe of Manasseh left the rest of Israel at Shiloh in the land of Canaan. They started the journey back to their own land of Gilead, the territory that belonged to them according to the LORD's command through Moses.

But while they were still in Canaan, and when they came to a place called Geliloth near the Jordan River, the men of Reuben, Gad, and the half-tribe of Manasseh stopped to build a large and imposing altar.

The rest of Israel heard that the people of Reuben, Gad, and the half-tribe of Manasseh had built an altar at Geliloth at the edge of the land of Canaan, on the west side of the Jordan River. So the whole community of Israel gathered at Shiloh and prepared to go to war against them. First, however, they sent a delegation led by Phinehas son of Eleazar, the priest, to talk with the tribes of Reuben, Gad, and the half-tribe of Manasseh. In this delegation were ten leaders of Israel, one from each of the ten tribes, and each the head of his family within the clans of Israel.

When they arrived in the land of Gilead, they said to the tribes of Reuben, Gad, and the half-tribe of Manasseh, "The whole community of the LORD demands to know why you are betraying the God of Israel. How could you turn away from the LORD and build an altar for yourselves in rebellion against him? Was our sin at Peor not enough? To this day we are not fully cleansed of it, even after the plague that struck the entire community of the LORD. And yet today you are turning away from following the LORD. If you rebel against the LORD today, he will be angry with all of us tomorrow.

"If you need the altar because the land you possess is defiled, then join us in the LORD's land, where the Tabernacle of the LORD is situated, and share our land with us. But do not rebel against the LORD or against us by building an altar other than the one true altar of the LORD our God. Didn't divine anger fall on the entire community of Israel when Achan, a member of the clan of Zerah, sinned by stealing the things set apart for the LORD? He was not the only one who died because of his sin."

Then the people of Reuben, Gad, and the half-tribe of Manasseh answered the heads of the clans of Israel: "The LORD, the Mighty One, is God! The LORD, the Mighty One, is God! He knows the truth, and may Israel know it, too! We have not built the altar in treacherous rebellion against the LORD. If we have done so, do not spare our lives this day. If we have built an altar for ourselves to turn away from the LORD or to offer burnt offerings or grain offerings or peace offerings, may the LORD himself punish us.

"'The truth is, we have built this altar because we fear that in the future your descendants will say to ours, 'What right do you have to worship the LORD, the God of Israel? The LORD has placed the Jordan River as a barrier between our people and you people of Reuben and Gad. You have no claim to the LORD.' So your descendants may prevent our descendants from worshiping the LORD.

"So we decided to build the altar, not for burnt offerings or sacrifices, but as a memorial. It will remind our descendants and your descendants that we, too, have the right to worship the LORD at his sanctuary with our burnt offerings, sacrifices, and peace offerings. Then your descendants will not be able to say to ours, 'You have no claim to the LORD.'

"If they say this, our descendants can reply, 'Look at this copy of the Lord's altar that our ancestors made. It is not for burnt offerings or sacrifices; it is a reminder of the relationship both of us have with the Lord.' Far be it from us to rebel against the Lord or turn away from him by building our own altar for burnt offerings, grain offerings, or sacrifices. Only the altar of the Lord our God that stands in front of the Tabernacle may be used for that purpose."

When Phinehas the priest and the leaders of the community—the heads of the clans of Israel—heard this from the tribes of Reuben, Gad, and the half-tribe of Manasseh, they were satisfied. Phinehas son of Eleazar, the priest, replied to them, "Today we know the Lord is among us because you have not committed this treachery against the Lord as we thought. Instead, you have rescued Israel from being destroyed by the hand of the Lord."

Then Phinehas son of Eleazar, the priest, and the other leaders left the tribes of Reuben and Gad in Gilead and returned to the land of Canaan to tell the Israelites what had happened. And all the Israelites were satisfied and praised God and spoke no more of war against Reuben and Gad.

The people of Reuben and Gad named the altar "Witness," for they said, "It is a witness between us and them that the Lord is our God, too" (Joshua 22:9-34 NLT).

Two and a half tribes on the east side (east-siders) of the Jordan River wanted a memorial in the form of an altar to remind both their descendants and the descendants of the west-siders that they were both Israelites who worshipped God. They feared that the natural border of the river would cause the people to separate over time.

The other tribes, the west-siders, assumed these east-siders had set up an altar to replace the worship of God at the tabernacle, so they prepared for war.

However, some of the wise people from the east side sent out representatives from each tribe to find out why the altar was being built. When they heard the truth, they were both embarrassed and thankful they had not attacked first and asked questions later.

To avoid an embarrassing fall, don't jump to conclusions without having any evidence. Take the time you need to investigate and then evaluate the truth you find. Going to war for a phantom reason will leave a lot of carnage that could have otherwise been spared.

Mind Reading

In Genesis chapters 11-25, one of the best-known couples in the Bible, Abraham and Sarah, serve as reminders of what happens when we presume to know God's plans, and the plans of others. This couple often strayed from God's will. Early on they gave into fear, dishonesty, and manipulation as they dealt with others. At times they wrongly presumed to know God's mind and plans before He had revealed them and then foolishly attempted to assist Him.

The good news is, over time Abraham and Sarah got the lesson. They learned that a fresh start is always possible. They also learned that the fulfillment of God's promises does not depend upon our performance, but rather on His grace. Finally, they learned it is dangerous to try to read God's mind and to move ahead without first seeking His direction.

This mind reading trap assumes that you know what the other person is thinking or expecting, or that you expect another person to fully understand what you're thinking.

Mind reading often happens when we know or think we know the other person well. After forty years of being married to my wife, she's learned she can't always read my mind.

The way to avoid the trap of assuming you know what another person is thinking is to ask questions. Getting answers is the easiest way to see if what you are thinking matches what the other person is thinking. It takes courage, but it can work.

Here are a few questions to ask:

- ❖ Did I express myself?

- ❖ Did I ask for information and clarification?

- ❖ Am I sure the other person isn't holding anything back in fear of my reaction?

Me, Me, Me

The third trap is believing you are the sole cause of every problem you encounter. But this is contrary to everything the apostle Paul teaches in Ephesians 2:1-13 (NLT).

Once you were dead because of your disobedience and your many sins. You used to live in sin, just like the rest of the world, obeying the devil—the commander of the powers in the unseen world. He is the spirit at work in the hearts of those who refuse to obey God.

All of us used to live that way, following the passionate desires and inclinations of our sinful nature. By our very nature we were subject to God's anger, just like everyone else.

But God is so rich in mercy, and he loved us so much, that even though we were dead because of our sins, he gave us life when he raised Christ from the dead. (It is only by God's grace that you have been saved!)

For he raised us from the dead along with Christ and seated us with him in the heavenly realms because we are united with Christ Jesus. So God can point to us in all future ages as examples of the incredible wealth of his grace and kindness toward us, as shown in all he has done for us who are united with Christ Jesus.

God saved you by his grace when you believed. And you can't take credit for this; it is a gift from God. Salvation is not a reward for the good things we have done, so none of us can boast about it. For we are God's masterpiece. He has created us anew in Christ Jesus, so we can do the good things he planned for us long ago.

Don't forget that you Gentiles used to be outsiders. You were called "uncircumcised heathens" by the Jews, who were proud of their circumcision, even though it affected only their bodies and not their hearts. In those days you were living apart from Christ. You were excluded from citizenship among the people of Israel, and you did not know the covenant promises God had made to them.

You lived in this world without God and without hope. But now you have been united with Christ Jesus. Once you were far away from God, but now you have been brought near to him through the blood of Christ.

This Scripture passage shows us a proven way out of the stinking thinking trap of thinking everything is our fault. The key verse for overcoming this trap is verse 10: "For we are God's masterpiece. He has created us anew in Christ Jesus, so we can do the good things he planned for us long ago." The challenge for a growing believer is to realize this truth and to be actively involved in allowing it to transform his or her life.

Some people are so Me, Me, Me that they blame themselves for a bus crash in Bangladesh. They think if they had prayed more or harder or better, then the crash wouldn't have happened.

I see so many people get stuck in this trap. Each one believes he or she is the sole problem in every relationship. Everything that goes wrong is his or her fault. A person who turns every event inward sucks the life out of those around him or her. If you believe you are the sole cause of every problem you've ever encountered, the action step is to look outside yourself. Ask yourself how others and/or circumstances may have contributed to the situation.

Them, Them, Them

The next automatic negative thought or stinking thinking trap is Them, Them, Them—believing that other people or circumstances are the cause of every problem you encounter. Jesus had something to say about this.

"Do not judge others, and you will not be judged. For you will be treated as you treat others. The standard you use in judging is the standard by which you will be judged.

"And why worry about a speck in your friend's eye when you have a log in your own? How can you think of saying to your friend, 'Let me help you get rid of that speck in your eye,' when you can't see past the log in your own eye? Hypocrite! First get rid of the log in your own eye; then you will see well enough to deal with the speck in your friend's eye" (Matthew 7:1-5 NLT).

This stinking thinking trap has been around since man first walked the earth. In Genesis 3 the Lord gave Adam a charge to be accountable, but instead he blamed his wife for their sin.

Sometimes we avoid dealing with our own stuff by evaluating and criticizing others. Jesus instructs us to look at our imperfections before we censor and condemn the faults in others.

I work with people who have anger management issues. When one of these people starts a sentence with "My wife..." "My husband..." "My boss..." or "My mama..." I smile and wait. Then I'll say, "Wow. So you have absolutely zero control over your emotions? You're being completely controlled by external circumstances? People, aliens, the government, the president, the economy, your congressman, your girlfriend, your boyfriend, your mom, your dad—it's all their fault? Are you sure all of these are against you and that you're helpless and hopeless?"

My wife has a wonderful business. She's involved with Premier Designs Jewelry. It has been a lifesaver for her because it has had a positive impact emotionally, mentally, and financially to our family. She has overcome the negative impact of growing up in an abusive home. While struggling with depression, she refused to give in to it. Her self-esteem, love for God, and her leadership skills have grown. I'm so proud of what she's done. She works hard. She has a dream. She's a leader. She encourages other women to have a dream and to move beyond their past hurts.

You know what's sad? People get excited about business, but many don't want to do business. I know people in the counseling profession who really want to help people. They spend thousands of dollars and years training for their degree and they go out into the world and hang their sign up and nobody shows up. Part of what I do in my counseling practice is try to help therapists realize that as a therapist, you have to let people know you're available and that you're unique. In other words, you have to work to find work.

In the direct-selling business with Premier Designs Jewelry, we see lots of ladies get into the business and they get excited, at first. They start out wanting to have a successful business. They ask a few people to have a home show or to invite people over for a party and nobody shows up, or maybe their husband isn't supportive, so they decide to quit after a few negative responses. If asked why they quit, they typically say, "Well, none of my friends will buy. Or nobody will do this or that. People are against me. The culture is against me. The economy is against me."

They find an external source to blame for failure. We've become a society of professional complainers and blamers. If we find the right person to blame, we feel justified in blaming people for our problems. Unfortunately, today there are therapists who make a lot of money helping people find ways to attach blame to someone else.

If you believe that other people or circumstances are the cause of every problem you encounter, then you need to look inward. That's right. Take that journey inside and ask yourself this critical question: How did I contribute to this?

Greg Terrell and his wonderful wife, Melissa, are senior leaders and excellent trainers with Premier Jewelry. At a training event, Greg said, "Many people who get into the business tell me they can't sell anything."

Greg simply replies, "Ladies, if you show the jewelry, people will buy it."

If you don't show your jewelry, if you don't tell people about your business, if people don't know what you do, then they're not going to spend their money.

If your life isn't going well, then you need to determine what you have done to contribute to the situation. If you have problems with personal boundaries, then lack of boundaries contributes to other people taking advantage of you. If you never stand up for yourself, then your reticence contributes to your lack of success. If you don't do your job, then your boss may reprimand you or terminate your job. Look inward and discover how you contribute to the problem, and then begin to take some positive steps to stop.

Always, Always, Always

Do you believe that negative events are unchangeable and you have little or no control over them? If so, you've fallen into the Always, Always, Always trap.

Gideon fell into this trap. When the angel of the Lord declared him a mighty warrior, Gideon was quick to remind the angel that he was a loser and if God was so strong, then why was Israel in shambles?

> The angel of the LORD appeared to him and said, "Mighty hero, the LORD is with you!"

> "Sir," Gideon replied, "if the LORD is with us, why has all this happened to us? And where are all the miracles our ancestors told us about? Didn't they say, 'The LORD brought us up out of Egypt'? But now the LORD has abandoned us and handed us over to the Midianites."

> Then the LORD turned to him and said, "Go with the strength you have, and rescue Israel from the Midianites. I am sending you!"

> "But Lord," Gideon replied, "how can I rescue Israel? My clan is the weakest in the whole tribe of Manasseh, and I am the least in my entire family!"

The Lord said to him, "I will be with you. And you will destroy the Midianites as if you were fighting against one man."

Gideon replied, "If you are truly going to help me, show me a sign to prove that it is really the Lord speaking to me. Don't go away until I come back and bring my offering to you."

He answered, "I will stay here until you return."

Gideon hurried home. He cooked a young goat, and with a basket of flour he baked some bread without yeast. Then, carrying the meat in a basket and the broth in a pot, he brought them out and presented them to the angel, who was under the great tree.

The angel of God said to him, "Place the meat and the unleavened bread on this rock, and pour the broth over it." And Gideon did as he was told. Then the angel of the Lord touched the meat and bread with the tip of the staff in his hand, and fire flamed up from the rock and consumed all he had brought. And the angel of the Lord disappeared.

When Gideon realized that it was the angel of the Lord, he cried out, "Oh, Sovereign Lord, I'm doomed! I have seen the angel of the Lord face to face!"

"It is all right," the Lord replied. "Do not be afraid. You will not die." And Gideon built an altar to the Lord there and named it Yahweh-Shalom (which means "the Lord is peace"). The altar remains in Ophrah in the land of the clan of Abiezer to this day (Judges 6:12-24 NLT).

Have you ever thought you were destined to bondage, poverty, and failure? When we get caught up in this stinking thinking trap, we slowly give up on the possibility of change. The action step is to grab control. Granted, you may not control your entire environment, but there are components you can and need to control. You need to lean into that.

Ask yourself these questions:

- ❖ What is changeable?
- ❖ What can I control?
- ❖ How should I go about doing so?

If you answer these questions, you will begin to push back on Always, Always, Always. Then the power you've given the negativity in your life can be transformed into a positive.

Everything, Everything, Everything

Do you believe you can judge a person's worth, motivation, or ability on the basis of a single situation? A person who falls into the Everything, Everything, Everything trap believes we have superhuman ability to understand everybody's motivation and ability. If you tend to evaluate and critique people and situations, ask yourself one critical question: What specific behavior explains the situation?

Let's look at 2 Kings 5:9-14 (NLT) to figure this out.

So Naaman went with his horses and chariots and waited at the door of Elisha's house. But Elisha sent a messenger out to him with this message: "Go and wash yourself seven times in the Jordan River. Then your skin will be restored, and you will be healed of your leprosy."

But Naaman became angry and stalked away. "I thought he would certainly come out to meet me!" he said. "I expected him to wave his hand over the leprosy and call on the name of the LORD his God and heal me! Aren't the rivers of Damascus, the Abana and the Pharpar, better than any of the rivers of Israel? Why shouldn't I wash in them and be healed?" So Naaman turned and went away in a rage.

But his officers tried to reason with him and said, "Sir, if the prophet had told you to do something very difficult, wouldn't you have done it? So you should certainly obey him when he says simply, 'Go and wash and be cured!'" So Naaman went down to the Jordan

River and dipped himself seven times, as the man of God had instructed him. And his skin became as healthy as the skin of a young child's, and he was healed!

Naaman was the commanding general of the armies of what is now known as Syria. He was a powerful military and political figure, a man of wealth, position, and power. He also had a diagnosis of leprosy, which meant he lost everything.

He heard about a prophet in Israel who might be able to heal him. He located the prophet, who told him to dip himself seven times in the Jordan River if he wanted to be healed. Naaman was furious. He thought his own power and authority were enough. In the end, he realized he wasn't right about everything, he acknowledged his lack of control and power, dipped himself seven times, and was healed. Naaman believed he could effectively judge both the prophet and the prophet's instruction because the rivers were better back home and he was a man of power. Fortunately, members of his team persuaded him to reconsider, and he was healed.

Stand on the Word

None of these solutions are easy. While it is simple to identify your thinking style or styles, the real work of changing them can be a daunting task. If they were easy, we could start a business and get rich. Identifying and stopping these stinking thinking traps takes time, energy, and effort, but the reward is great because when you begin to realize you have power, faith, talents, strengths, gifts, and resources, you will be able to make the necessary changes. The apostle Paul reminds us that we "can do everything through Christ" (Philippians 4:13).

One of the ways we change stinking thinking is by reprogramming our computer—our brain. We do that by starting with the Word of God.

I'd like to share three portions of Scripture with you.

The first is Psalm 130:5: "I'm counting on the LORD; yes, I'm counting on him. I have put my hope in his word."

The second comes from Isaiah 61:1, "The spirit of the Sovereign LORD is upon me, for the LORD has anointed me to bring good news to the poor. He has sent me to comfort the brokenhearted and to proclaim that captives will be released and prisoners will be freed."

This verse in Isaiah is one of the verses that the Lord Jesus quoted when He entered his public ministry. As you're dealing with challenges of any sort—from depression or anxiety to low self-esteem—I want you to hear this and realize that part of what the Lord wants to do for you is in this verse. Think about that for a minute.

If you're feeling brokenhearted, beat up, depressed, rejected, downtrodden, discouraged, if you're feeling lower than a pregnant ant, Jesus said He's come to comfort you. Doesn't hearing how much He cares make your burden feel a little lighter?

Hiding the Word of God in our heart is the way we combat automatic negative thoughts. The third verse is 2 Timothy 1:7, "For God has not given us a spirit of fear and timidity, but of power, love, and self-discipline." Read that verse again. God's given us more than we realize, but we have to give those muscles of power, love, and self-discipline a workout.

Changing your thought life will not be easy. The labor of "renewing your mind" (Romans 12:2) involves more than thinking happy thoughts. It involves a completely new way of viewing yourself, your world, and your future. You are uniquely loved by God, accountable to Him, and especially precious and valuable to Him. At the same time, the Bible makes it clear that as sinful people, we all engage in erroneous thinking that comes from a different point of view (Romans 1:21, 28). Consequently, the job of relearning how to think biblically goes beyond becoming more rational or realistic. The goal and purpose of a follower of Jesus is to learn how to think with the mind of Christ (2 Corinthians 10:5), to have the same attitudes Jesus had (Philippians 2:5).

ATC Practice Example

Activating event: Your credit card is declined at the store.

Thoughts: What are some of your automatic, initial thoughts?

_____

_____

_____

_____

What is your behavioral reaction to your thoughts?

_____

_____

_____

_____

Consequences: Is your reaction helpful or harmful? Please describe.

_____

_____

_____

_____

Avoid the Stinking Thinking Traps Practice

Did you notice any stinking thinking traps in your answers? Work with a partner and place a checkmark next to any traps you notice. Your partner will ask the appropriate critical question (see below) to identify important information you might have overlooked. Record any new information beneath the question.

Jumping to Conclusions

❖ Slow down: Do I have any evidence to show I have been wronged or am I jumping the gun?

_____

_____

_____

Mind Reading

❖ Speak Up: Did I express myself fully so the other person didn't need to try to read my mind? Or did I ask for information from the other person rather than attempting to read his or her mind?

_____

_____

_____

Me, Me, Me

❖ Look outward: How did others or circumstances contribute to my current situation?

_____

_____

_____

_____

Them, Them, Them

❖ Look inward: How did I control or fuel my situation?

_____

_____

_____

_____

Always, Always, Always

❖ Grab control: What can I change? What can I influence?

_____

_____

_____

_____

Everything, Everything, Everything

❖ Look at behavior: What specific behavior explains my situation?

_____

_____

_____

_____

Chapter 5

Getting Better

There is a dirty little secret of biological psychiatry and of clinical psychology—they have both given up on the notion of finding a cure for depression.[29] Curing depression, when it can be done, takes too long. And since most insurance companies will only cover brief treatment, patients cannot receive the amount of treatment they need.[30] Therapy and drugs are basically about short-term crisis management and about prescribing cosmetic treatments.

There are two kinds of drugs: cosmetic medications and curative drugs.[31] If you take an antibiotic long enough, it will kill the bacterial invaders and you will be cured. When you finish the course of treatment, that disease will not recur because the germs that caused it have been killed. Quinine is a medication for malaria. When you take it, you get temporary suppression of the symptoms. If you stop taking the medication, the symptoms return.

According to Dr. Marty Seligman, a popular author, professor of psychology and director of the Positive Psychology Center at the University of Pennsylvania, every single drug on the shelf of psych pharmacopoeia is cosmetic.[32] The effect of managed care and the expense of mental health have seduced psychology and psychiatry into working on symptom relief, not on a cure.

The second little secret is that the combination of medication and psychotherapy only relieves depression 80 percent of the time.

Considerable research had gone into trying to identify which therapies, or combination of therapies, are most effective in treating most mood disorders. Taking an average of the research literature on these two treatment options, you get a 65 percent relief rate, accompanied by a placebo effect that ranges from 45 to 55 percent. The more realistic and elaborate the placebo, the higher the placebo percentage; so high is the placebo response that in half of the officially approved U.S. Food and Drug Administration (FDA) studies of antidepressant drugs, there was no difference between placebo and the drugs.[33]

Realistically, we measure how effective traditional talk therapies and medical treatment are by how long the treatment lasts before the patient has a meltdown or an episode once treatment is completed.

If you are stuck, it might be time make a change in how you are treating depression. The field of positive psychology fused with a biblical worldview helps you learn to manage depression in a more meaningful way. Dr. Shelly Gable, assistant professor of psychology at the University of California, has developed the Active and Constructive Responding Model. [34] This model shows that how we respond to a given situation can either make it better or worse.

I have my own adaptation—an expansion of the glass is half empty or half full point of view.

There are four basic ways to respond to a given situation. As we examine a couple of situations, keep in mind that the active and constructive response is the best way to respond.

Situation #1

Your wife has been working hard on her home-based business and she has received an email from her company's home office telling her she has been promoted. She is excited as she tells you about the news.

Here are four possible responses:

- ❖ Active and Constructive: "Outstanding! I am so proud of you. I know how hard you have worked. Why don't we go out and celebrate and you can tell me all about it." (Nonverbal communication: Maintaining eye contact, displays of positive emotions, such as genuine smiling, touching, laughing.)

❖ Passive and Constructive: "That is good news." (Nonverbal communication: Little or no active emotional expression. No eye contact. Little or no physical contact.)

❖ Active and Destructive: "That sounds like a lot to take on. Does that mean you are going to be more involved in your business and less involved with me and the children?" (Nonverbal communication: Displays of negative emotions, such as a furrowed brow, frowning, eye rolling, or pouting.)

❖ Passive and Destructive: "What are we doing Friday night?" (Nonverbal communication: Little or no eye contact, turning away, leaving the room without any acknowledgment of her accomplishment.)

Situation # 2

On your way home from work, you stop by your local convenience store for some gas and a Coke Zero™, and with the change you do something you never do—you pick up a couple of lottery tickets. The first one is a bust, but you win $100 on the second ticket. You resist the temptation to call your wife and gloat, but she knows something is up when you barge into the kitchen. "I won $100 on a lottery ticket!"

Active and Constructive: "Wow, aren't you the lucky guy? Sweet! How did you feel when you realized you were a winner?" (Nonverbal communication: Maintaining eye contact, displays of positive emotions, such as genuine smiling, touching, laughing.)

❖ Passive and Constructive: "Cool." (Nonverbal communication: Little or no active emotional expression. No eye contact. Little or no physical contact.)

❖ Active and Destructive: "I hope you don't have a gambling addiction." (Nonverbal communication: Displays of negative emotions, such as a furrowed brow, frowning, eye rolling, or pouting.)

❖ Passive and Destructive: "You will probably blow it." (Nonverbal communication: Little or no eye contact, turning away, leaving the room without any acknowledgment.)

Do you get the idea?

One of the things I routinely do in my counseling practice, even with patients who are having a rough time, is to ask them to tell me about one positive event that happened in the past week. At first, they look a little surprised, but they usually lighten up and tell me a good story.

Here is your task for the week: Listen each time someone you care about tells you about something good that happened to him or her. Do your best to respond actively and constructively. Don't go overboard with too much enthusiasm; be honest and genuine in your positive response. Next, ask the person to recreate the event with you. The more time he or she spends remembering the story, the better. Be on the lookout all week for positive events, recording them each evening in the following format:

❖ Other Person's Positive Event
❖ My Response
❖ Other Person's Response to Me

If you aren't good at such things, then plan ahead. Jot down concrete positive events that you have heard about recently. Write down how you should have responded. When you get up the next morning, spend about five minutes visualizing who you will encounter that day and what good things they are likely to share with you. Pre-plan your active, constructive response. Try using variations on this theme all week. You will be surprised at the results.

This tool is self-maintaining. It does not come naturally to most of us, so practice it for three or four weeks and watch how you and others change. Warning: This will make you feel better.

Once you begin to adjust to how you interact with others using this tool, others will like you more, they will want to spend more time with you, and they will share more with you. The byproduct: You will feel better about yourself.

Engaging the Negative Emotions

In the past hundred years the therapist's job has usually had something to do with minimizing negative emotions—prescribing medications, providing techniques and interventions that make people less angry, anxious, and depressed. Reducing these emotions isn't easy and even though parents, pastors, and teachers have picked up this torch, many people aren't able to simply stop the negative emotions. The more realistic and hopeful approach is to learn to function well, even when you are sad, mad, or anxious.

New personality research has shown that personality traits are highly heritable, which can indicate that a person may have genetically inherited a strong predisposition to sadness, joy, anxiety, or being spiritually minded.[35] Dysphoria, an emotional state characterized by anxiety, depression, or uneasiness, often, but not always, stems from personality traits. Powerful biological and neurological underpinnings influence some people to sadness, anxiety, and anger. Therapists can modify these emotions, but only within limits.

What are some practical implications from inherited traits?

If I am a born pessimist, even though I know some truth, even though I go to a church, or even if I receive professional therapy, I will still hear the voice that whispers, "I am a failure," and "I will never get it." You learn to turn that voice down, but it will always be there, lurking in the background, randomly whispering those automatic negative thoughts.

Don't give up hope. It is going to get better.

Abraham Lincoln and Winston Churchill had lifelong struggles with depression. They were both highly functioning leaders who gave great direction and leadership in times when their nations were involved in life-and-death struggles, while at the same time dealing with their own "black dog"[36] and suicidal thoughts. Both had to learn to adapt, adjust, and overcome.

Churchill was born into a family with a history of mental illness. During Churchill's lifetime his father displayed psychotic symptoms, and

Winston's daughter Diana, who had a major depressive episode in 1952, ultimately died by suicide in 1963.

However, it was Churchill's own illness, which he referred to as his "black dog," that played a major role in World War II and Churchill's career development. Some suspect that it was Churchill's recurrent episodes of depression that allowed him to realistically assess the threat of Germany. Because of his depression, he may have understood that simply conciliating Hitler would not stop Germany from advancing across Europe. [37]

Here is the truth, no matter how good we clinicians are: You will still wake up sometimes feeling blue and thinking life is hopeless. Your job is not only to fight those feelings, but also to live heroically, functioning well even on the bad days. Hold on to the truth found in Romans 8:35-39 (NLT):

> Can anything ever separate us from Christ's love? Does it mean he no longer loves us if we have trouble or calamity, or are persecuted, or hungry, or destitute, or in danger, or threatened with death? (As the Scriptures say, "For your sake we are killed every day; we are being slaughtered like sheep.") No, despite all these things, overwhelming victory is ours through Christ, who loved us.
>
> And I am convinced that nothing can ever separate us from God's love. Neither death nor life, neither angels nor demons, neither our fears for today nor our worries about tomorrow—not even the powers of hell can separate us from God's love. No power in the sky above or in the earth below—indeed, nothing in all creation will ever be able to separate us from the love of God that is revealed in Christ Jesus our Lord.

Medications and various therapies can and do help, but for the most part they serve as symptomatic relievers. Consequently, specific, successful preparation in dealing with depression and functioning well, even in the presence of symptoms, must be a serious part of recovery and therapy.

Another way of looking at this is to become more resistant to depression, anxiety, and anger. The term "resistance" may be defined as "the ability of an individual to resist manifestations of clinical depression, distress, sadness, and impairment." Resistance can be thought of as a type of psychological, spiritual, and behavioral immunity to distress and dysfunction.

But treatment should not end when symptoms are reduced. The client needs to develop specific skills that will help him or her have more positive energy, more engagement, a stronger sense of accomplishment, and a better sense of connection with the Lord and others.

Unlike the clinical skills of minimizing symptoms, pain, and misery, these skills both help treat and prevent depression and anxiety. Even more important than pushing back pathology, these skills will help you thrive and are a pivotal part of the search for meaning.

Good News

Forty percent of your happiness and outlook is under your direct voluntary control and can be increased by the types of activities you engage in and in your outlook on life.[38] No matter what your background or life story, there is a lot you can do to influence your level of happiness.

Dr. Marty Seligman has developed a broad model based on his lifetime of study of human behavior, which he calls the "Well-Being Theory."[39]

According to his book *Flourish*, the well-being theory has five elements: positive emotion (hope for the present and future, emphasis mine), engagement, meaning, positive relationships, and accomplishment.

Seligman divides these five components into the mnemonic PERMA.

POSITIVE EMOTION. My personal view is that this has to do with one's overall subjective view of life. As a growing Christian, positive emotion has more to do with a working knowledge that God loves me and has a purpose for my life. This understanding enhances my faith and gives me hope for both the present and the future.

ENGAGEMENT. Well-being includes a sense that life is purpose-filled, more pleasurable than painful, and that we experience pleasure, comfort, ecstasy, warmth, companionship, and love.

RELATIONSHIPS. Positive and uplifting connections with others, whether through church, work, neighborhoods, the military, community organizations, family, and friends are the best antidote to the ups and downs of life. Being connected has multiple positive benefits. Some of these benefits include preventing or minimizing the impact of depression and stress, increasing self-esteem, building a feeling of connectedness, and building community.

For centuries, churches have provided small groups for Bible study, life issues, and challenges, as well as short-term service projects. These intimate gatherings allow people the power to live life together in a world that is increasingly disconnected from eyeball-to-eyeball, skin-on-skin relationships.

While no system is perfect, Seligman and his disciples provide fresh tools to help us get a snapshot of our progress. Here is a formula to get a sense of your well-being.

MEANING. This is a sense that I belong to and serve something/someone bigger than myself.

ACCOMPLISHMENT/ACHIEVEMENT. Having specific goals in life, even little ones, is important to well-being and happiness. Reaching goals, checking items off your bucket list, and experiencing levels of success in life build self-esteem and provide a sense of accomplishment.

My view is that we need a note of caution here because winning for winning's sake, that is for the sole purpose of wealth, is a dead end. In Matthew 16:26 (NLT) Jesus said, "And what do you benefit if you gain the whole world but lose your own soul...?" On the other hand, people who live in a free society have the opportunity to dream and to do the work to fulfill those dreams. When we are able to work on fulfilling our destiny, finding and living our passion, then we will feel that sense of accomplishment. People who lead the achieving life are often absorbed in what they do, pursue pleasure avidly, and feel positive emotion (however evanescent) when they win, and may win in service of something larger. Do you remember the movie *The Chariots of Fire* (1981)? It is a great movie about two Olympians, Eric Liddell, a devout Christian who ran for the glory of God, and Harold Abrahams, a Jew who ran to overcome prejudice. One of the notable quotes from the film is when the actor portraying Liddell says, "God made me fast, and when I run, I feel his pleasure."

Subjective Well-being (SWB)
SWB = SWL + HPA + LNA

The model for subjective well-being combines the way you think about happiness (cognitive) with how you feel about it (emotional).

SWL stands for satisfaction with life. This factor is how you rate your current life compared to your idealized life. Thus, a big disconnect from where you are now and your ideal results in low life satisfaction.

HPA stands for high positive effect and refers to experiencing positive emotions. HPA is more about how often you experience joy and other positive emotions, rather than intensity.

LNA is the exact opposite; it represents the low negative affect—the total of your experience of negative emotions.

A positive subjective well-being (SWB) requires the amount of positive effect to be higher than the negative effect.

The formula works when the following five elements are incorporated into well-being. As you read through this checklist, take note about how you are doing in each one. If you check all of them off, you are probably in a good place. If you find that you are low in any of these areas, it is an indication of an area in which you might need to do some work.

☐ **Self-acceptance:** Accepting yourself for you who are without any external expectations.

☐ **Positive relationships:** Having good relations with people is vital for a meaningful life. While social media and the Internet provide multiple levels of interaction between people, it is not the same as being in the same space, sharing life together.

☐ **Life purpose/meaning:** Connecting your goals, direction, and feelings to something bigger than yourself.

☐ **Accomplishment/achievement:** Achieving and accomplishing ambitions, dreams, goals, and aspirations.

☐ **Autonomy:** Having a sense of personal control in thought and action.

As we wrap up this portion of the book, I'd like to invite you to consider doing two things.

First, perform a random act of kindness for someone. Buy a cup of coffee for someone. Let a senior citizen cut in line. Let someone merge into traffic.

Second, carry a pad of paper or a small journal with you. As you go through your day, notice the world around you and make a list in the journal of everything you see that makes you thankful. Did the sun shine brightly through the windows? Did you hear a baby laugh? Did a smell remind you of a happy time? Write each one on your list. As you count the blessings of the day, you'll be happier and less depressed.

Simple Things You Can Do to Push Back Depression

Depression robs you by making you feel inadequate and worthless. As bad as robbery sounds, you and I always have choices in how we respond to what life throws at us.

One of the things you can do for yourself is to focus on what you appreciate about your life, yourself, and your situation. While this is a simple concept, it may be a difficult task, particularly if you have been under the heaviness of depression. Part of getting better is to begin to stop speaking the nagging, negative thoughts that so easily slip into your mind when you are depressed.

Stop Saying Bad Things About Yourself

In place of negative thoughts and words, try noticing what you do appreciate about yourself. No matter how bad you feel, there are good things about you.

Try this assignment. Make a list of at least seven things that you appreciate. Here are a few suggestions to consider adding to your list:

> A good listener
>
> A good read
>
> A loyal friend
>
> A fresh, warm chocolate chip cookie
>
> A hug
>
> A good workout

The purpose of this exercise is to help you begin to push back the dark, consuming, negative thoughts and focus on the good around you.

I love the line from Kathryn Stockett's *The Help*, "You is kind. You is smart. You is important." These are keeper phrases because you are all of those and more.

Recently, I heard Jennifer Rothschild, a talented speaker and author who has devised a clever tool to help push back negative thoughts. Ten words for ten fingers that can help you move in a positive direction. Here is the verbiage, "I can do all things through Christ who strengthens me." Now put the book down, face the palms of your hands up and begin with your left hand moving right, "I can do all things through Christ who strengthens me." What a great tip, and it is simple and your fingers are always available as a prop.

Summary:

1. Stop repeating the negative.

2. Make a list of the positives.

3. Carry your list with you. (Hint: If you write it out on paper, you are more likely to use it.)

Quit Comparing

Depression, by its nature, fogs up your sense of self. When you are struggling in the negative swill of depression, it can be easy to find other people who are doing better in nearly every area of life. To combat this darkness, you stop comparing yourself to others. There will always be someone with better looks, more money, and greater status than you, but you do not have to be sucked into the trap of comparison.

Instead, choose to catch yourself the next time you begin to compare yourself to others. When one of those comparative thoughts starts, stop it, and replace it with one or two positive things about yourself.

Be deliberate about noticing what is good. "And now dear brothers and sisters, one final thing. Fix your thoughts on what is true, and honorable, and right, and pure, and lovely, and admirable (Philippians 4:8 NLT).

Bump up your positive experiences

Sasha had been volunteering as the women's ministry director in her church for the past three years. She led the ministry through the ups and downs including power struggles and emotional drama. She spent hours in prayer and in personal study. The other night she told her husband, Leo, that she thought she was done.

For the next half hour she cried, complained, and released all the frustrations that had built up. Leo was wise that night. He said, "Do you need a hug?" The next morning Sasha asked Leo what she should do. Once again he wisely said, "Call a couple of your girlfriends and go have some fun."

She did. She and two of her girlfriends spent some Kohl's bucks and then went to Starbucks.

One of the classic effects of depression is stealing your sense of pleasure. Without some pleasurable experiences woven into your life, you can descend into the dull grayness of depression.

Being intentional about having pleasurable experiences is one way to overcome the low motivation that can be a part of depression.

Here is one proven plan for boosting your pleasure.

Do this:

1. Record every activity you do for the next three to five days.

2. Answer the following question for each activity: Was it pleasurable? Yes or No?

3. For each pleasurable activity, rate it from 1 to 10 -- 1 being the least pleasurable and 10 being the most.

Re-energize

Depression will sap your energy, but you choose how you respond to it.

One of the best ways to re-energize your self is to monitor your mouth. Depressed people tend to talk depressed using sad words and sad tones—much like Eeyore.

Using negative language when you talk to yourself, especially when you consistently feel helpless and hopeless, is a sure-fire way to keep feeling depressed. Multiple studies on negative self-talk show how gloomy and unhelpful words and thoughts increase depression and anxiety. Making small changes in the way you verbalize can have an enormous, positive impact on the way you feel. And the best thing about this idea, it doesn't cost a penny. Here are a couple of examples.

You can feel better if you drop the phrase "I can't." Instead, try saying, "I won't." This tiny shift in language, changing one four-letter word for another, can have a huge positive impact on your mood. Learn to say it loud and proud.

Instead of saying, "I can't get out of bed," say, "I won't get up in the morning."

106

"I can't feel enthusiastic about my business," becomes, "I won't become enthusiastic about my business."

These small shifts in your verbiage will have a powerful impact on how you feel. When you do this, you move from a position of impotence and powerlessness into choice, which opens up possibilities. When you make this subtle shift, what you are really saying is, "My thoughts and my actions are under my control." Those nine words make a powerful statement.

Step Back from the Problem

When Thomas Edison felt stumped by a problem, he removed himself from the work area, lay down, and took a little nap. Years before the research on power napping was available, he understood the importance to stepping back from a problem to get a better perspective. Taking a break from the problem results in a fresh perspective.

There are ways to put this principle into practice.

1. Stop. Quit putting needless energy into solving a problem that isn't getting solved.

2. Do something completely different. Choose to swim, go for a walk, take a break, call a friend, pray, read the Bible. It should be a repetitive activity that gets your undivided attention and absorbs, redirects, and gives you energy. Ten to twenty minutes is usually enough time to reset.

3. Observe what happens about the issue when you return your thoughts to it.

Stop Isolating

Isolation is the double-edged sword of depression as it is both a cause and an outcome. Isolation complicates depression in some people, particularly in those who are socially isolated and do not normally turn outward for relief. Individuals begin drinking, gambling online, using pornography, or beginning other addictions to treat their depression.

Over the years I've had a few clients like Reggie who struggled with his severe, recurrent depression and his ten-year battle with alcohol abuse. He consistently complained about how lonely he was but minimized how much he was drinking by himself. He tried church support groups, Alcoholics Anonymous, going to the gym with friends, but each program seemed to fail miserably. Alcohol kept him from overcoming the isolation. Reggie eventually dealt with his addiction and then he began to recover from the depression.

So how do you move out of isolation?

For people with significant depression, the mere thought of getting out of the house can seem daunting. Here is an action plan that you can begin using today.

1. Connect Intentionally

Get up and get dressed. Go outside; take a walk. Let the sun kiss your cheeks. As you walk, observe people, children, and pets.

Nod your head and say, "Hi," on purpose. The point is not to start a conversation but to make a brief moment of connection. This link may sound insignificant, but it isn't. Stepping out of your house or apartment and intentionally speaking are two fundamental ways of changing your perception. You will see that you are not a zombie-like presence in the world. Try this action plan daily.

2. Connect Online

Reaching out via email or some limited posting can be helpful in re-establishing contact with others. For people with depression there are some risks to communicating over the Internet and social media. Be careful to safeguard your personal information and keep your expectations real. Start small.

3. Join a Group or Class.

In your community there are numerous organizations that center around a common goal. Perhaps you enjoy photography, sports, games, exercise, biking, writing, reading, poetry, animals, or genealogy. One local library even has an old movie night. Read the local newspaper or go online looking for activities in your community and join. The connection with others will help relieve the pain of isolation.

4. Plan to Meet with One or More Persons.

As you connect with others, take a risk and invite one person to meet you at a local coffee shop or restaurant. When you arrive, smile, make eye contact, shake hands, and ask the person questions about his or her life. As you learn about and connect with this person, your feelings of isolation will go away.

Isolation is not your friend, but you can get trapped into being alone. Instead, embrace your responsibility to take action and push through isolation.

Work on Balance

Achieving balance is critical to breaking the bonds of depression. When I ride a bicycle, I am constantly trying to stay balanced. All of the small and large muscle groups work together to keep the bicycle and me in the upright position and going in the right direction. Balance takes work. You can begin attaining balance.

1. **Break Out of Your Rut**

   a. Take 100 percent responsibility for yourself. You and I hold the keys that can unlock the lock and release the chains that hold us back.
   b. Think, dream, and write down how you will feel better in the future.
   c. Move more – even a little bit of exercise has positive benefits.
   d. Read books that put good, healthy thoughts in your brain. Try more self-help and Christian living and less fiction.

2. **Remember and repeat past joyful, fulfilling experiences.** Begin by remembering, looking at photos, and reflecting on good things. Read through and work on the Experience Gratitude section.

3. **Re-embrace your relationship with God.** Jesus loves you more than you will ever know, and He specializes in working with

people who feel messed up and disconnected. Take a moment; ask Him to draw you close. Then don't be surprised when He does.

4. **Don't overplay the negative.** Overthinking the past does little to improve it. The rest of this resource is designed to give you practical, biblical tools to help you move toward hope and a renewed sense of purpose and intentional living.

Experience Gratitude

"Count your blessings, name them one by one. Count your blessings, see what God has done…" are words from a hymn I remember from my childhood while attending the First Baptist Church of Fort Valley. It is an old song with modern psychological and spiritual implications.

Gratitude makes your life happier and more satisfying. When we feel gratitude, we benefit from the pleasant memory of a positive event. In addition, when we express our gratitude to others, we strengthen our relationship with them.

The Gratitude Visit

An exercise called the Gratitude Visit will help you experience relief from depression.

Close your eyes. Imagine the face of someone still alive who did something or said something that changed your life for the better. Got a face?

Your task is to write a letter to this individual and deliver it in person. The letter should be concrete and about three hundred words; be specific about what they did for you and how it affected your life.

Once you have completed the letter, call the person and let them know that you would like to visit them, but be vague about the purpose of the meeting. This type of exercise is more fun when it is a surprise. When you meet with the individual, take your time reading your letter. Notice their reactions as well as yours. If they interrupt you, gently tell them that you want them to listen until you are done. I promise you that you and the recipient will be much happier and less depressed.

Savor

To savor something is to taste or smell it. Think about this for a minute. Which do you think a person tends to savor more, a steak served at a buffet or a cooked-to-order steak at a nice steak house paid for by someone else? I bet you'd savor that gourmet steak and consume it slowly.

One of the easiest tools we use as we continue to look at ways to overcome depression is to savor pleasant memories; past answers to prayer; a meaningful Scripture verse; and positive, meaningful words spoken to you. When we purposely reflect and meditate on these types of good, positive things, our brains begin to move toward health.

Allow the Lord to Restore Your Soul.

As you continue your journey to wholeness and as you continue to actively participate in pushing back depression by using some of the tools that I have outlined in this book may I remind you of the Shepherd's Psalm?

Psalm 23

The Lord is my shepherd;

I have all that I need.

He lets me rest in the green meadows;

he leads me beside peaceful streams.

He renews my strength.

He guides me along right paths,

bringing honor to his name.

Even when I walk

through the darkest valley,

I will not be afraid,

for you are close beside me.

Your rod and your staff

protect and comfort me.

You prepare a feast for me

in the presence of my enemies.

You honor me by anointing my head with oil.

My cup overflows with blessings.

Surely your goodness and unfailing love will pursue me

All the days of my life,

and I will live in the house of the Lord

forever.

NLT

Chapter 6

Bible Study

Lesson 1: Coming to Terms with Hopelessness

Susan was a twenty-five year old who had an emergency hysterectomy following the birth of her first child, who was stillborn. In addition to the loss of her child, Susan was painfully aware of the loss of ever having children who were biologically her own. In Susan's emotional experience, these losses meant the loss of all hope for future happiness.

Being the mother of John's children was what Susan wanted more than anything else in life. To lose this ability felt like losing everything. When friends tried to cheer her up with reminders of her successful career or with thoughts of adoption, Susan felt even more alone with her hopelessness. The future stretched out in front of her like a bleak desert. She was unable to dream that life would ever feel good again.

Hopelessness is giving up on the future and is fundamentally a spiritual struggle. When we believe all hope is gone, we wonder if God is a good God. Does God care?

The text for this study examines a day full of feelings of hopelessness. The day Jesus was crucified. All hope must have disappeared for His followers. They had looked to Him for deliverance from their oppressors and for a better future. He was the Messiah in whom they had placed all their faith, trust, and aspirations. Now He was dead. The world had gone mad. They wondered why and how God could allow such a thing to happen. What hope could there possibly be in the face of this evil?

Personal Reflection

Think about a time when you felt hopeless. Write about that time below. Please be specific.

_____

_____

_____

_____

_____

_____

_____

What events seem to trigger experiences of decreased hope?

_____

_____

_____

_____

_____

_____

_____

_____

What has helped you make it through times of hopelessness?

_____

_____

_____

_____

_____

_____

_____

_____

Get a Grip on Scripture

Read Matthew 27:41-56 (NLT).

The leading priests, the teachers of religious law, and the elders also mocked Jesus. "He saved others," they scoffed, "but he can't save himself! So he is the King of Israel, is he? Let him come down from the cross right now, and we will believe in him! He trusted God, so let God rescue him now if he wants him! For he said, 'I am the Son of God.'" Even the revolutionaries who were crucified with him ridiculed him in the same way.

At noon, darkness fell across the whole land until three o'clock. At about three o'clock, Jesus called out with a loud voice, "Eli, Eli, lema sabachthani?" which means "My God, my God, why have you abandoned me?"

Some of the bystanders misunderstood and thought he was calling for the prophet Elijah. One of them ran and filled a sponge with sour wine, holding it up to him on a reed stick so he could drink. But the rest said, "Wait! Let's see whether Elijah comes to save him."

Then Jesus shouted out again, and he released his spirit. At that moment the curtain in the sanctuary of the Temple was torn in two, from top to bottom. The earth shook, rocks split apart, and tombs opened. The bodies of many godly men and women who had died were raised from the dead. They left the cemetery after Jesus' resurrection, went into the holy city of Jerusalem, and appeared to many people.

The Roman officer and the other soldiers at the crucifixion were terrified by the earthquake and all that had happened. They said, "This man truly was the Son of God!"

And many women who had come from Galilee with Jesus to care for him were watching from a distance. Among them were Mary Magdalene, Mary (the mother of James and Joseph), and the mother of James and John, the sons of Zebedee.

As you think about what you've read in this passage, did you see any phrases or words that gave you a new awareness or understanding?

_____

_____

_____

_____

_____

_____

_____

_____

_____

_____

_____

_____

_____

_____

The religious leaders and the criminals mocked Jesus as he was dying, saying, "He trusts in God. Let God rescue him now if he wants him!" Yet God did not rescue him. Then Jesus cried out to God, "Why have you forsaken me?" Describe a time in your life when you felt like God had forsaken you.

_____

_____

_____

_____

_____

_____

When you feel forsaken by God, how does this affect your ability to experience hope?

_____

_____

_____

_____

_____

What thoughts and feelings do you have in response to everything that happened after Jesus died?

_____

_____

_____

_____

_____

Think of a situation which left you feeling hopeless but which turned out to be a time of significant growth or positive change in your life. What happened to make you see things differently?

_____

_____

_____

_____

_____

How might it help you to remember that Jesus experienced a time of hopelessness?

_____

_____

_____

_____

_____

How might it help you to know that God is at work, even in your times of hopelessness?

_____

_____

_____

_____

_____

Write a prayer. What would you like to say to God about your experience of hopelessness?

_____

_____

_____

_____

_____

Lesson 2: Longing for Hope

Without hope, we do not care what happens to us. We withdraw from others; we no longer feel pleasure; we have no interest in going about our daily lives; sometimes a lack of hope leads to thoughts of suicide.

When depression becomes intense, it is difficult to remember that life once seemed meaningful or to imagine that life could ever feel worthwhile again. We have no past, no future, just the intensely painful present. And the waiting. We're not sure exactly what we are waiting for. Are we waiting for something to change? For the rage and despair to dissipate? For God to speak?

Waiting for hope to materialize is one of the most difficult parts of recovery from depression. No matter how long this period lasts, it is a stage that seems to last too long. The process seems pointless to our conscious mind (Why can't we do something?). But depression is a battle at the spiritual core of our being. Transformation is slow and cannot be hurried. If God spoke too soon, it would seem like more words added to the clamor of the friends and family who have spoken too soon, too glibly, and too cheerfully. Waiting for God is the necessary part of our healing journey.

The text for this study is about how the prophet Jeremiah waited for God. Jeremiah was deeply depressed after his people were taken into exile and his city was destroyed. Everything he knew and loved was lost. He sat in the ashes of the destruction and wept. He wept for his friends and for his city. And he wept for himself. God provided the first glimmer of hope for Jeremiah in the midst of his deepest grief. It was only a glimpse, but it was enough.

Personal Reflection

Sometimes it is difficult to allow the possibility of hope into our thoughts. What barriers make it difficult for you to allow for the possibility of hope?

_____

_____

_____

_____

_____

Think of a time when you were surprised by something good that you had not allowed yourself to hope for. What happened? How did you feel?

_____

_____

_____

_____

_____

Get a Grip on Scripture

Read Lamentations 3:16-24 (NLT).

He has made me chew on gravel.

He has rolled me in the dust.

Peace has been stripped away,

and I have forgotten what prosperity is.

I cry out, "My splendor is gone!

Everything I had hoped for from the LORD is lost!"

The thought of my suffering and homelessness

is bitter beyond words.

I will never forget this awful time,

as I grieve over my loss.

Yet I still dare to hope

when I remember this:

The faithful love of the LORD never ends!

His mercies never cease.

Great is his faithfulness;

his mercies begin afresh each morning.

I say to myself, "The LORD is my inheritance;

therefore, I will hope in him!"

What facts did you see in this passage? What was a new idea or perspective you hadn't thought of before?

_____

_____

_____

_____

_____

_____

_____

Restate in your own words how the prophet describes his depression.

_____

_____

_____

_____

_____

This text begins with the prophet's experience of disappointment with God. The prophet blames God for the terrible things that have happened. What does the prophet say God has done?

_____

_____

_____

_____

_____

How might believing that God has caused his suffering have contributed to Jeremiah's hopelessness?

_____

_____

_____

_____

_____

The prophet also makes statements of hope. Restate in your own words what Jeremiah says gave him hope.

_____

_____

_____

_____

_____

What new thoughts and feelings do you have in response to Jeremiah's perspective about God's love?

_____

_____

_____

_____

_____

An obvious tension between hope and despair exists in this text. How is it possible to believe God has failed you or hurt you and yet still find hope in Him?

_____

_____

_____

_____

_____

The prophet says, "I will wait for him." Describe what you think it means to wait for God when your sense of hope is fragile.

_____

_____

_____

_____

_____

_____

When you are struggling with hopelessness, how can you wait for God? Be specific.

_____

_____

_____

_____

_____

_____

God's gifts of compassion are new every morning. Picture yourself sitting on a mountainside, facing east across a valley, looking at another mountain range. The sky that has been dark for a long time is growing light. Even though you cannot see the sun, you know it is rising behind the distant mountains. A new day is about to dawn. Listen to God say, "I have new gifts of love for you today." What thoughts and feelings do you have in response to this picture?

_____

_____

_____

_____

Write a prayer. What would you like to say to the God whose compassion never fails?

_____

_____

_____

_____

_____

_____

Lesson 3: Making Room for Hope

Bill spent months grieving his losses. He lost his childhood because he grew up in an alcoholic home. He grieved over more recent losses in relationships he had formed as an adult. Sometimes, his life felt like one long depression session.

His grief gradually led to him being able to focus on the reality of the losses and to experience his feelings about them, but he described this season as an emotional roller coaster. Sometimes he was surprised by how much better he felt and then, just as quickly, he plunged back into deep depression. The emotional ups and downs confused him.

"I guess I'm not sure I want to let go of my depression," he said. "This really must sound crazy, I know, but the depression is all I have left to show that I really value the relationships I have lost. What I lost was important to me. I'm afraid that if I am not in pain, it will mean that I didn't really care or that I don't care anymore."

Hanging onto depression is a normal and predictable part of recovery. It is not crazy. People often believe that if they give up their depression, they will have nothing left. But as recovery progresses, people begin to feel other emotions coming back to life. In the text for this study we see the psalmist beginning to make room for hope in the midst of his depression.

Personal Reflection

Think of a time when you were aware of God's love and care for you. Describe the situation.

_____

_____

_____

_____

How did you experience God's care in the situation?

_____

_____

_____

_____

_____

How might remembering this experience contribute to your sense of hope?

_____

_____

_____

_____

_____

Get a Grip on Scripture

Read Psalm 77:1-20 (NLT).

I cry out to God; yes, I shout.
Oh, that God would listen to me!
When I was in deep trouble,
I searched for the Lord.
All night long I prayed, with hands lifted toward heaven,
but my soul was not comforted.
I think of God, and I moan,
overwhelmed with longing for his help. Interlude
You don't let me sleep.
I am too distressed even to pray!

I think of the good old days,
long since ended,
when my nights were filled with joyful songs.
I search my soul and ponder the difference now.
Has the Lord rejected me forever?
Will he never again be kind to me?
Is his unfailing love gone forever?
Have his promises permanently failed?
Has God forgotten to be gracious?
Has he slammed the door on his compassion? Interlude
And I said, "This is my fate;
the Most High has turned his hand against me."
But then I recall all you have done, O LORD;
I remember your wonderful deeds of long ago.
They are constantly in my thoughts.
I cannot stop thinking about your mighty works.
O God, your ways are holy.
Is there any god as mighty as you?
You are the God of great wonders!
You demonstrate your awesome power among the nations.
By your strong arm, you redeem your people,
the descendants of Jacob and Joseph. Interlude
When the Red Sea saw you, O God,
its waters looked and trembled!
The sea quaked to its very depths.
The clouds poured down rain;
the thunder rumbled in the sky.
Your arrows of lightning flashed.
Your thunder roared from the whirlwind;
the lightning lit up the world!
The earth trembled and shook.
Your road led through the sea,
your pathway through the mighty waters—
a pathway no one knew was there!
You led your people along that road like a flock of sheep,
with Moses and Aaron as their shepherds.

What did you see in this passage that interested you or caused you to wonder?

_____

_____

_____

_____

_____

How does the psalmist describe his depression?

_____

_____

_____

_____

_____

The psalmist says that his "soul was not comforted." What do you think the psalmist meant by this?

_____

_____

_____

_____

_____

_____

What might cause a person to believe he or she does not want to be comforted?

_____

_____

_____

_____

_____

Restate in your own words the questions the psalmist asks of God. (See verses 7-9)

_____

_____

_____

_____

_____

What questions have you asked God when you have been depressed?

_____

_____

_____

_____

_____

_____

The questions we ask God when we are depressed are urgent questions. What is the relationship between these questions and our search for hope?

_____

_____

_____

_____

_____

_____

The psalmist's struggle with depression leads him to actively seek hope by meditating on God's mighty deeds; in this way, the psalmist begins to make room for hope. Restate in your own words some of the truths about God from the psalmist's reflections. How might considering God's powerful interventions on behalf of His people help increase our capacity for hope?

_____

_____

_____

_____

_____

_____

Which of the psalmist's statements about God is particularly meaningful to you?

_____

_____

_____

_____

Explain why it is meaningful.

_____

_____

_____

_____

_____

_____

Write a prayer. What would you like to say to God about your desire to make room for hope?

_____

_____

_____

_____

_____

_____

Lesson 4: Receiving Gifts of Hope

When we are depressed, we lose interest in the simple pleasures of life. We don't have the energy to feel appropriate feelings of gratitude when someone gives us a gift. Depression sucks the joy right out of us. Instead of experiencing gratitude, we may wonder if a gift is supposed to make us feel better or if the giver of the gift has forgotten how much pain we feel.

In the process of healing and recovering from depression, however, we renew our capacity to receive simple gifts like companionship, food, and sleep. Depression may have deprived us of these things, and we must learn afresh how to be with others and how to nourish our bodies with food and sleep.

In the text for this study the prophet Elijah has been threatened with death because he has challenged the worship of the god Baal. Elijah knows that the threats are serious. Therefore, he flees in fear, alone, to the desert. There he sinks into a deep depression. As the text shows, God finds ways to bring gifts of hope to Elijah in the midst of his depression.

Personal Reflection

Think of a time when you were depressed and someone gave you a gift (companionship, dinner, love) that you were able to receive. What did he or she do?

_____

_____

_____

_____

_____

How was it helpful?

_____

_____

_____

_____

_____

What are some of the gifts of caring that are especially meaningful to you when you are depressed?

_____

_____

_____

_____

_____

How do these gifts of caring contribute to your ability to hang on to hope?

_____

_____

_____

_____

_____

_____

Get a Grip on Scripture

Read 1 Kings 19:3-9 (NLT).

Elijah was afraid and fled for his life. He went to Beersheba, a town in Judah, and he left his servant there. Then he went on alone into the wilderness, traveling all day. He sat down under a solitary broom tree and prayed that he might die. "I have had enough, Lord," he said. "Take my life, for I am no better than my ancestors who have already died."

Then he lay down and slept under the broom tree. But as he was sleeping, an angel touched him and told him, "Get up and eat!" He looked around and there beside his head was some bread baked on hot stones and a jar of water! So he ate and drank and lay down again.

Then the angel of the Lord came again and touched him and said, "Get up and eat some more, or the journey ahead will be too much for you."

So he got up and ate and drank, and the food gave him enough strength to travel forty days and forty nights to Mount Sinai, the mountain of God. There he came to a cave, where he spent the night.

But the Lord said to him, "What are you doing here, Elijah?"

What happened in this passage? Does any part of this event seem strange to you?

_____

_____

_____

_____

_____

How does Elijah express his hopelessness in words? How does Elijah express his hopelessness in his actions?

_____

_____

_____

_____

_____

Elijah ran for his life because of threats to kill him. The threats followed a series of events in which Elijah had risked a great deal and God had used him in powerful ways. What circumstances increase the risk that you will experience depression?

_____

_____

_____

_____

_____

How would you compare your experiences of depression with Elijah's?

_____

_____

_____

_____

_____

What significance do you see in the gifts the angel brought to Elijah in his time of depression?

_____

_____

_____

_____

_____

Picture yourself in Elijah's situation. Alone. Afraid. Exhausted. Hunted. Giving up on life. Now picture someone bringing you simple, thoughtful gifts. Homemade bread. Cool, clear water. Companionship. Picture yourself receiving these gifts. What thoughts and feelings do you have in response to this image?

_____

_____

_____

_____

_____

What gift do you need most at this time?

_____

_____

_____

_____

_____

How might it help you to believe that God wants to give you the good gifts you need?

_____

_____

_____

_____

_____

Write a prayer. What would you like to say to God about your need for gifts of hope?

_____

_____

_____

_____

_____

_____

Lesson 5: Growing Toward Hope

Mary's long and intense struggle with depression began five years ago, when she moved to a new city. Today, over lunch with her best friend, Mary reviewed the last five years.

"If I could go back in time," she mused, "and choose whether or not to go through this, I wouldn't hesitate for a minute, even though I would never choose to experience what I have experienced. I have grown enormously as a person because of this struggle. I am more compassionate now, less judgmental, and more attentive to emotional pain." She paused. "But no growth in my character could ever make up for the pain of this struggle. Don't get me wrong, I am grateful for the growth that has come. I'm glad I've grown. But I'm not glad for the losses or for the emotional pain."

Depression can be an opportunity for emotional and spiritual growth. Growth comes through the most surprising circumstances. Growth does not mean that depression is good; it does not mean that we choose to go through this experience. Growth comes in the midst of recovery, however. Growth is progress and improvement. God is able to take the pain and evil in our lives and turn it into something good and meaningful. He is able to exchange beauty for ashes (Isaiah 61:3). And for that, we can be grateful.

Personal Reflection

What positive qualities of character have your struggles helped to develop in you?

_____

_____

_____

_____

How have the positive changes impacted your relationship with God? With friends? With people at work? With your family?

_____

_____

_____

_____

_____

_____

Get a Grip on Scripture

Read Romans 5:1-8 (NLT).

Therefore, since we have been made right in God's sight by faith, we have peace with God because of what Jesus Christ our Lord has done for us. Because of our faith, Christ has brought us into this place of undeserved privilege where we now stand, and we confidently and joyfully look forward to sharing God's glory.

We can rejoice, too, when we run into problems and trials, for we know that they help us develop endurance. And endurance develops strength of character, and character strengthens our confident hope of salvation. And this hope will not lead to disappointment. For we know how dearly God loves us, because he has given us the Holy Spirit to fill our hearts with his love.

When we were utterly helpless, Christ came at just the right time and died for us sinners. Now, most people would not be willing to die for an upright person, though someone might perhaps be willing to die for a person who is especially good. But God showed his great love for us by sending Christ to die for us while we were still sinners.

What understanding did you gain from this passage?

_____

_____

_____

_____

_____

What does this text say about the source of peace and hope?

_____

_____

_____

_____

_____

According to this text, if we rejoice in our sufferings—not because our sufferings are good, but because they lead to hope—hope doesn't disappoint us. What is your response to this suggestion?

_____

_____

_____

_____

How might suffering produce perseverance and character?

_____

_____

_____

_____

_____

We can rejoice when we run into problems and trials, for
we know they help us develop endurance. And endurance
develops strengths of character, and character strengthens our
confident hope of salvation.

How might growth in our character increase our capacity for hope?

_____

_____

_____

_____

_____

This text says that hope will not disappoint us. "For we know how dearly God loves us, because he has given us the Holy Spirit to fill our hearts with his love." What is the relationship between experiencing God's love and experiencing hope?

_____

_____

_____

Hope is both a gift of love that we receive and something we grow toward. What experiences have you had with receiving hope which led to the further growth of hope?

_____

_____

_____

_____

_____

_____

What does this text tell us about God's love?

_____

_____

_____

_____

_____

_____

Picture your heart as a beautiful, well-crafted bowl. It has been carved deep by your suffering and made strong by God's gifts of care. Picture God pouring His love, in the form of crystal clear water, into your bowl. His love fills your heart to overflowing. You hear God saying to you, "I love you. I have always loved you. I will always love you." How do you respond to this picture?

_____

_____

_____

_____

Write a prayer. What would you like to say to God about your journey of growing toward hope?

_____

_____

_____

_____

_____

_____

Lesson 6: The Source of Hope

My mom and dad failed me," Linda said in her support group meeting. "Then my marriage fell apart. And then my health fell apart. Life has always been hard. I don't see why I should expect it to ever get any better. If anything, it will probably get worse. How is it possible for me to have hope? Life seems to come with a guarantee of hardships and suffering."

Human relationships seem to be accompanied with disappointment and loss. Many of us have echoed Linda's question. How is it possible to have hope? If hope is the expectation of good, how can we experience hope when we live on a fallen planet as fallen creatures? The Bible teaches that there is more to the story of our lives than our experiences of loss and disappointment. The planet may be fallen, but God does not forsake it. God is actively present in our lives, bringing gifts of life and joy into the midst of our darkness. We dare to hope because God is a God of love and compassion who actively cares for us.

Personal Reflection

What gifts of life and joy have you experienced in the midst of darkness?

_____

_____

_____

_____

_____

_____

_____

In what ways has your relationship with God been negatively impacted by your experiences with depression? Explain.

_____

_____

_____

_____

_____

_____

In what ways has your relationship with God been positively impacted by your experiences with depression? Explain.

_____

_____

_____

_____

_____

Get a Grip on Scripture

Read Psalm 146 (NLT)

Praise the LORD!

Let all that I am praise the LORD.

I will praise the LORD as long as I live.

I will sing praises to my God with my dying breath.

Don't put your confidence in powerful people;

there is no help for you there.

When they breathe their last, they return to the earth,

and all their plans die with them.

But joyful are those who have the God of Israel as their helper,

whose hope is in the LORD their God.

He made heaven and earth,

the sea, and everything in them.

He keeps every promise forever.

He gives justice to the oppressed

and food to the hungry.

The LORD frees the prisoners.

The LORD opens the eyes of the blind.

The LORD lifts up those who are weighed down.

The LORD loves the godly.

The LORD protects the foreigners among us.

He cares for the orphans and widows,

but he frustrates the plans of the wicked.

The LORD will reign forever.

He will be your God, O Jerusalem, throughout the generations.

Praise the LORD!

How did you feel when you read this passage?

_____

_____

_____

_____

_____

_____

The psalmist mentions eight kinds of circumstances that might seem hopeless. List these situations/conditions and the reasons they might seem hopeless.

1. _____

2. _____

3. _____

4. _____

5. _____

6. _____

7. _____

8. _____

How did God respond in each of these situations?

_____

_____

_____

_____

_____

_____

What do God's responses to people in hopeless situations suggest to you about God's character?

_____

_____

_____

_____

Which of the eight images of hopelessness do you most strongly relate to at this time? Explain.

_____

_____

_____

_____

_____

_____

Take a few minutes and allow yourself to picture God responding to you in the way this text describes. What thoughts and feelings do you have in response to this image of God's care for you?

_____

_____

_____

_____

_____

_____

Write a brief psalm of your own, thanking God for being your help and your hope.

_____

_____

_____

_____

_____

_____

Write a prayer. What would you like to say to God who is the source of your hope?

_____

_____

_____

_____

_____

_____

Additional Scriptures for Study

Read Mark 2:17 (NLT)

When Jesus heard this, he told them, "Healthy people don't need a doctor—sick people do. I have come to call not those who think they are righteous, but those who know they are sinners."

According to the Lord's own words, does it show lack of faith to receive help from a physician? Why or why not?

_____

_____

_____

_____

_____

_____

∽

Read Psalm 42 (NLT)

As the deer longs for streams of water,
so I long for you, O God.
I thirst for God, the living God.
When can I go and stand before him?
Day and night I have only tears for food,
while my enemies continually taunt me, saying,
"Where is this God of yours?"
My heart is breaking

as I remember how it used to be:
I walked among the crowds of worshipers,
leading a great procession to the house of God,
singing for joy and giving thanks
amid the sound of a great celebration!
Why am I discouraged?
Why is my heart so sad?
I will put my hope in God!
I will praise him again—
my Savior and my God!
Now I am deeply discouraged,
but I will remember you—
even from distant Mount Hermon, the source of the Jordan,
from the land of Mount Mizar.
I hear the tumult of the raging seas
as your waves and surging tides sweep over me.
But each day the LORD pours his unfailing love upon me,
and through each night I sing his songs,
praying to God who gives me life.
"O God my rock," I cry,
"Why have you forgotten me?
Why must I wander around in grief,
oppressed by my enemies?"
Their taunts break my bones.
They scoff, "Where is this God of yours?"
Why am I discouraged?
Why is my heart so sad?
I will put my hope in God!
I will praise him again—
my Savior and my God!

What would you say was the psalmist's problem? What did he recognize as the one major attitude he was missing to help him overcome this problem?

_____

_____

_____

_____

_____

_____

∽

Read Mark 3:17 (NLT)

James and John (the sons of Zebedee, but Jesus nicknamed them "Sons of Thunder")

Analyze the description given James and John in this verse. What kind of emotional energy did they show at times?

_____

_____

_____

_____

_____

∽

Read Job 30 (NLT)

List some of his symptoms of depression, as seen in the following verses:

30:1 "But now I am mocked by people younger than I, by young men whose fathers are not worthy to run with my sheepdogs."

_____

_____

_____

_____

30:15 "I live in terror now. My honor has blown away in the wind, and my prosperity has vanished like a cloud."

_____

_____

_____

_____

30:22 "You throw me into the whirlwind and destroy me in the storm."

_____

_____

_____

_____

_____

30:23 "And I know you are sending me to my death—the destination of all who live."

_____

_____

_____

_____

30:28 "I walk in gloom, without sunlight. I stand in the public square and cry for help."

_____

_____

_____

_____

❧

Read Job 42:1-10 (NLT)

Then Job replied to the LORD: "I know that you can do anything, and no one can stop you. You asked, 'Who is this that questions my wisdom with such ignorance?' It is I—and I was talking about things I knew nothing about, things far too wonderful for me. You said, 'Listen and I will speak! I have some questions for you, and you must answer them.'

I had only heard about you before, but now I have seen you with my own eyes. I take back everything I said, and I sit in dust and ashes to show my repentance."

After the Lord had finished speaking to Job, he said to Eliphaz the Temanite: "I am angry with you and your two friends, for you have not spoken accurately about me, as my servant Job has. So take seven bulls and seven rams and go to my servant Job and offer a burnt offering for yourselves. My servant Job will pray for you, and I will accept his prayer on your behalf. I will not treat you as you deserve, for you have not spoken accurately about me, as my servant Job has." So Eliphaz the Temanite, Bildad the Shuhite, and Zophar the Naamathite did as the Lord commanded them, and the Lord accepted Job's prayer.

When Job prayed for his friends, the Lord restored his fortunes. In fact, God gave him twice as much as before!

Job's life turned around when God led him to change his focus. In these verses, what attitude of Job's was the turning point? What steps can you take to similarly focus your attention, attitudes, goals, and outlook so they are in tune with what God desires for your life?

_____

_____

_____

_____

_____

_____

❧

Read Psalm 42:3-4 (NLT)

Day and night I have only tears for food,
while my enemies continually taunt me, saying,
"Where is this God of yours?"
My heart is breaking
as I remember how it used to be:
I walked among the crowds of worshipers,
leading a great procession to the house of God,
singing for joy and giving thanks
amid the sound of a great celebration!

Describe the psalmist's emotional state. If you have ever felt this way, what were the circumstances?

_____

_____

_____

_____

_____

_____

∽

Read Psalm 42:5-6 (NLT)

Why am I discouraged?
Why is my heart so sad?
I will put my hope in God!

I will praise him again—

my Savior and my God!

Now I am deeply discouraged,

but I will remember you—

even from distant Mount Hermon, the source of the Jordan,

from the land of Mount Mizar.

How is the psalmist turning his feelings into words? Clue: He is verbalizing by talking out his feelings to_____(v. 5) and to_____(v. 6). Because we are reading his words, we assume that he probably committed his feelings to what other form?

_____

_____

ᕚ

Read 1 Peter 1:18-19 (NLT)

> For you know that God paid a ransom to save you from the empty life you inherited from your ancestors. And the ransom he paid was not mere gold or silver. It was the precious blood of Christ, the sinless, spotless Lamb of God.

From these verses, how can you determine your true personal worth to God?

_____

_____

_____

_____

❧

Read 1 Kings 19:4 (NLT)

Then he went on alone into the wilderness, traveling all day. He sat down under a solitary broom tree and prayed that he might die. "I have had enough, LORD," he said. "Take my life, for I am no better than my ancestors who have already died."

Which symptoms of depression can you identify in Elijah's life from this verse?

_____

_____

_____

_____

_____

❧

Read 1 Kings 19:5-6 (NLT)

Then he lay down and slept under the broom tree. But as he was sleeping, an angel touched him and told him, "Get up and eat!" He looked around and there beside his head was some bread baked on hot stones and a jar of water! So he ate and drank and lay down again.

What gradual corrective steps were provided for him?

_____

_____

_____

_____

_____

_____

∽

Read 1 Kings 19:10-14 (NLT)

Elijah replied, "I have zealously served the LORD God Almighty. But the people of Israel have broken their covenant with you, torn down your altars, and killed every one of your prophets. I am the only one left, and now they are trying to kill me, too."

"Go out and stand before me on the mountain," the LORD told him. And as Elijah stood there, the LORD passed by, and a mighty windstorm hit the mountain. It was such a terrible blast that the rocks were torn loose, but the LORD was not in the wind. After the wind there was an earthquake, but the LORD was not in the earthquake. And after the earthquake there was a fire, but the LORD was not in the fire. And after the fire there was the sound of a gentle whisper. When Elijah heard it, he wrapped his face in his cloak and went out and stood at the entrance of the cave.

And a voice said, "What are you doing here, Elijah?"

He replied again, "I have zealously served the LORD God Almighty. But the people of Israel have broken their covenant with you, torn down your altars, and killed every one of your prophets. I am the only one left, and now they are trying to kill me, too."

What were some additional corrective steps that were provided for him?

_____

_____

_____

_____

_____

_____

∽

Read 1 Kings 19:15-16, 19 (NLT)

Then the LORD told him, "Go back the same way you came, and travel to the wilderness of Damascus. When you arrive there, anoint Hazael to be king of Aram. Then anoint Jehu grandson of Nimshi to be king of Israel, and anoint Elisha son of Shaphat from the town of Abel-meholah to replace you as my prophet . . .

So Elijah went and found Elisha son of Shaphat plowing a field. There were twelve teams of oxen in the field, and Elisha was plowing with the twelfth team. Elijah went over to him and threw his cloak across his shoulders and then walked away.

What gradual corrective steps were provided for him?

_____

_____

_____

_____

_____

_____

Get a Grip Personal Project

Moses, David, and Jonah also sometimes became depressed. Look at the following passages and ask yourself the following questions.

Read Numbers 11:10-17 (NLT)

Moses heard all the families standing in the doorways of their tents whining, and the LORD became extremely angry. Moses was also very aggravated. And Moses said to the LORD, "Why are you treating me, your servant, so harshly? Have mercy on me! What did I do to deserve the burden of all these people? Did I give birth to them? Did I bring them into the world? Why did you tell me to carry them in my arms like a mother carries a nursing baby? How can I carry them to the land you swore to give their ancestors? Where am I supposed to get meat for all these people? They keep whining to me, saying, 'Give us meat to eat!' I can't carry all these people by myself! The load is far too heavy! If this is how you intend to treat me, just go ahead and kill me. Do me a favor and spare me this misery!"

Then the LORD said to Moses, "Gather before me seventy men who are recognized as elders and leaders of Israel. Bring them to the Tabernacle to stand there with you. I will come down and talk to you there. I will take some of the Spirit that is upon you, and I will put the Spirit upon them also. They will bear the burden of the people along with you, so you will not have to carry it alone.

Who became depressed?

_____

Under what circumstances?

_____

Why was he depressed?

_____

How depressed?

_____

Significance to me?

_____

Solution for depression?

_____

_____

∽

Read Joshua 4 (NLT)

When all the people had crossed the Jordan, the LORD said to Joshua, "Now choose twelve men, one from each tribe. Tell them, 'Take twelve stones from the very place where the priests are standing in the middle of the Jordan. Carry them out and pile them up at the place where you will camp tonight.'"

So Joshua called together the twelve men he had chosen—one from each of the tribes of Israel. He told them, "Go into the middle of the Jordan, in front of the Ark of the

LORD your God. Each of you must pick up one stone and carry it out on your shoulder—twelve stones in all, one for each of the twelve tribes of Israel. We will use these stones to build a memorial. In the future your children will ask you, 'What do these stones mean?' Then you can tell them, 'They remind us that the Jordan River stopped flowing when the Ark of the LORD's Covenant went across.' These stones will stand as a memorial among the people of Israel forever."

So the men did as Joshua had commanded them. They took twelve stones from the middle of the Jordan River, one for each tribe, just as the LORD had told Joshua. They carried them to the place where they camped for the night and constructed the memorial there.

Joshua also set up another pile of twelve stones in the middle of the Jordan, at the place where the priests who carried the Ark of the Covenant were standing. And they are there to this day.

The priests who were carrying the Ark stood in the middle of the river until all of the LORD's commands that Moses had given to Joshua were carried out. Meanwhile, the people hurried across the riverbed. And when everyone was safely on the other side, the priests crossed over with the Ark of the LORD as the people watched.

The armed warriors from the tribes of Reuben, Gad, and the half-tribe of Manasseh led the Israelites across the Jordan, just as Moses had directed. These armed men— about 40,000 strong—were ready for battle, and the LORD was with them as they crossed over to the plains of Jericho.

That day the LORD made Joshua a great leader in the eyes of all the Israelites, and for the rest of his life they revered him as much as they had revered Moses.

The LORD said to Joshua, "Command the priests carrying the Ark of the Covenant to come up out of the riverbed." So Joshua gave the command. As soon as the priests carrying the Ark of the LORD's Covenant came up out of the riverbed and their feet were on high ground, the water of the Jordan returned and overflowed its banks as before.

The people crossed the Jordan on the tenth day of the first month. Then they camped at Gilgal, just east of Jericho. It was there at Gilgal that Joshua piled up the twelve stones taken from the Jordan River.

Then Joshua said to the Israelites, "In the future your children will ask, 'What do these stones mean?' Then you can tell them, 'This is where the Israelites crossed the Jordan on dry ground.' For the LORD your God dried up the river right before your eyes, and he kept it dry until you were all across, just as he did at the Red Sea when he dried it up until we had all crossed over. He did this so all the nations of the earth might know that the LORD's hand is powerful, and so you might fear the LORD your God forever."

Who became depressed?

_____

Under what circumstances?

_____

_____

Why was he depressed?

How depressed?

Significance to me?

Solution for depression?

᪥

Read Psalm 32 (NLT)

Oh, what joy for those
whose disobedience is forgiven,
whose sin is put out of sight!
Yes, what joy for those
whose record the LORD has cleared of guilt,
whose lives are lived in complete honesty!
When I refused to confess my sin,
my body wasted away,
and I groaned all day long.
Day and night your hand of discipline was heavy on me.
My strength evaporated like water in the summer heat.
Interlude

Finally, I confessed all my sins to you
and stopped trying to hide my guilt.

I said to myself, "I will confess my rebellion to the LORD."

And you forgave me! All my guilt is gone. Interlude

Therefore, let all the godly pray to you while there is still time,

that they may not drown in the floodwaters of judgment.

For you are my hiding place;

you protect me from trouble.

You surround me with songs of victory. Interlude

The LORD says, "I will guide you along the best pathway for your life.

I will advise you and watch over you.

Do not be like a senseless horse or mule

that needs a bit and bridle to keep it under control."

Many sorrows come to the wicked,

but unfailing love surrounds those who trust the LORD.

So rejoice in the LORD and be glad, all you who obey him!

Shout for joy, all you whose hearts are pure!

Who became depressed?

_____

Under what circumstances?

_____

_____

Why was he depressed?

_____

How depressed?

_____

Significance to me?

_____

Solution for depression?

_____

❧

Read Acts 16:25 (NLT)

> Around midnight Paul and Silas were praying and singing
>
> hymns to God, and the other prisoners were listening.

After being beaten and thrown into jail, what form of self-talk did Paul and Silas choose to give a broader meaning to their situation?

_____

_____

_____

_____

_____

_____

❧

Read Psalm 15:1-2 (NLT)

> Who may worship in your sanctuary, LORD?
>
> Who may enter your presence on your holy hill?
>
> Those who lead blameless lives and do what is right,
>
> speaking the truth from sincere hearts.

What kind of self-talk does the psalmist say is used by the man who dwells in fellowship with the Lord?

_____

_____

_____

_____

_____

_____

∾

Read Philippians 4:11 (NLT)

Not that I was ever in need, for I have learned how to
be content with whatever I have.

A feeling of contentment was not automatic for Paul. What word describes the discipline necessary for him to develop contentment, whatever his circumstances?

_____

_____

_____

_____

_____

∾

Read Psalm 42:11 (NLT)

> Why am I discouraged?
> Why is my heart so sad?
> I will put my hope in God!
> I will praise him again—
> my Savior and my God!

Here the psalmist chose faith-oriented self-talk. What spiritual quality was he challenging himself to accept as he looked at his situation?

_____

_____

_____

_____

_____

≫

Read Hebrews 12:1-2 (NLT)

> Therefore, since we are surrounded by such a huge crowd of witnesses to the life of faith, let us strip off every weight that slows us down, especially the sin that so easily trips us up. And let us run with endurance the race God has set before us. We do this by keeping our eyes on Jesus, the champion who initiates and perfects our faith. Because of the joy awaiting him, he endured the cross, disregarding

its shame. Now he is seated in the place of honor beside God's throne.

What was the mental focus the Lord Jesus chose in enduring the cross?

_____

_____

_____

_____

_____

_____

Appendix

Suicide: Knowing the Risk

Most people who commit suicide are depressed, but what pushes a person to this irreversible step varies from person to person. Depression of this magnitude comes from intense feelings of anger, despair, hopelessness, or panic. Sometimes the normally unthinkable can be carried out under the influence of highly distorted thinking or psychosis.

Most suicides are impulsive—meaning the time between the decision to kill oneself and the actual act is a few minutes to an hour. The emotional pain that leads to a suicidal crisis is often temporary (a job loss or the end of a romantic relationship). Experts have found that the toughest part of dealing with the emotional pain passes, and so does the urge to commit suicide.

A 2008 article in The New England Journal of Medicine stated that more than nine out of 10 people who attempted suicide and survived—even those who chose means that are often more lethal (such as shooting oneself in the head or jumping in front of a moving train)—don't die of suicide at a later date.

This information was validated in a study by the Center for Disease Control (CDC), which concluded that in the 15-24 age range, there are between 100 and 200 attempts for every completed suicide. Among adults 65 and older, there are approximately four attempts for every completed suicide. According to the CDC and the National Institute for Mental Health's "National Suicide Statistics at a Glance Report," there is one suicide every 15 minutes in the U.S.

Suicides rates vary by region, however, ranging from a high of one in 67 adults in Rhode Island to a low of one in 1,000 adults in Delaware and Georgia.

174

Overall, more than 2.2 million Americans reported making suicide plans in the past year and more than one million people actually attempted suicide. Suicide rates were consistently higher in the western states, and people in the Midwest and West were more likely to have had suicidal thoughts than those in the South.

"Multiple factors contribute to risk for suicidal behavior," said Linda C. Degutis, director of CDC's National Center for Injury Prevention and Control, in a press release. "The variations identified in this report might reflect differences in the frequency of risk factors and the social and economic makeup of the study populations. These differences influence the types of prevention strategies used in communities and the groups included."

The National Violent Death Reporting System includes information on the presence of alcohol and other substances. The finding from 16 states revealed that one-third of those who died of suicide tested positive for alcohol at the time of death and nearly one in five had evidence of opiates, including heroin and prescription pain killers.

Risk Factors for Suicide

Risk factors for thoughts of suicide vary with age, gender, and ethnic group. And risk factors often occur in combinations.

More than 90 percent of people who commit suicide have clinical depression or another diagnosable mental disorder. Some people who commit suicide have a substance abuse problem. Often they have that problem in combination with other mental disorders.

Adverse or traumatic life events in combination with other risk factors, such as clinical depression, may lead to suicide. But suicide and suicidal behavior are never normal responses to stress.

Other risk factors for suicide include:

- ❖ One or more prior suicide attempts
- ❖ Family history of mental disorder or substance abuse
- ❖ Family history of suicide

- ❖ Family violence
- ❖ Physical or sexual abuse
- ❖ Keeping firearms in the home
- ❖ Chronic physical illness, including chronic pain
- ❖ Incarceration
- ❖ Exposure to the suicidal behavior of others

Warning signs that someone may be thinking about or planning to commit suicide include:

- ❖ Always talking or thinking about death

- ❖ Clinical depression (deep sadness, loss of interest, trouble sleeping and eating) that gets worse

- ❖ Having a "death wish," tempting fate by taking risks that could lead to death, such as driving fast or running red lights

- ❖ Losing interest in things one used to care about

- ❖ Making comments about being hopeless, helpless, or worthless

- ❖ Putting affairs in order, tying up loose ends, changing a will

- ❖ Saying things like, "It would be better if I weren't here" or "I want out"

- ❖ Sudden, unexpected switch from being very sad to being very calm or appearing to be happy

- ❖ Talking about suicide

❖ Visiting or calling people to say goodbye

❖ Prior suicide attempts (According to the American Foundation for Suicide Prevention, between 20 and 50 percent of people who commit suicide have had a previous attempt.)

What you can do if you have suicidal thoughts:

❖ Talk with trusted friends, family members, or others you respect who can assist you

❖ Talk with your doctor, mental health professional, or pastor. Talking eases or removes suicidal urges. In some cases, though, hospitalization is necessary until a sense of balance is restored.

❖ Call the National Suicide Prevention Lifeline at 1-800-273-TALK (8255) or a local hotline to speak with a crisis counselor

Endnotes

1   Dweck, C.S., Mindset: *The New Psychology of Success*. New York: Random House (2006).

2   Yapko, M., *Breaking the Patterns of Depression*. New York Broadway Books (1997).

3   Miller, M., *Understanding Depression Special Health Report*. Boston: Harvard Medical School (2011).

4   Hendrick, B., "Use of Antidepressants on the Rise in the U.S." (2011) Retrieved April 13, 2012, http://www.webmd.com/depression/news/20111019/use-of-antidepressants-on-the-rise-in-the-us.

5   Ibid.

6   "What are the different forms of depression?" (2011). Retrieved April 13, 2012, from http://www.nimh.nih.gov/health/publications/depression/what-are-the-different-forms-of-depression.shtml

7   Seligman, M., *What You Can Change . . . and What You Can't*. New York: Random House (2006).

8   Ibid.

9   Ibid.

10   "What are the different forms of depression?" (2011). Retrieved April 13, 2012, from http://www.nimh.nih.gov/health/publications/depression/what-are-the-different-forms-of-depression.shtml

11   "Post Partum Depression," American Psychological Association (2012), Retrieved December 22, 2012, from http://www.apa.org/pi/women/programs/depression/postpartum.aspx#

12   Denis Mann, "Out of Blue." Originally written May 2005, accessed June 23, 2013. http://www.webmd.com/depression/postpartum-depression/features/brooke-shields-depression-struggle

13 "Seasonal Affective Disorder," Mayo Clinic Foundation for Medical Education and Research (2011). Retrieved April 12, 2012, from http://www.mayoclinic.com/health/seasonal-affective-disorder/DS00195/DSECTION=symptoms

14 Ibid.

15 "Bipolar Disorder," Retrieved November 17, 2012, from http://www.nimh.nih.gov/health/publications/bipolar-disorder-easy-to-read/complete-index.shtml

16 Miller, M., "Understanding Depression Special Health Report," (2011), Boston: Harvard Medical School, 19.

17 Simone, Lisa, "Jane Pauley: The Sanest Person on TV," accessed February 18, 2013, http://www.bphope.com/Item.aspx/196/jane-pauley-the-sanest-person-in-tv

18 Ibid.

19 Tan., S.Y., Ortberg, J., *Coping with Depression*. Grand Rapids: Baker Books (2004)

20 Coping with Chronic Illness and Depression (2011). Retrieved April 19, 2012, from http://www.webmd.com/depression/guide/chronic-illnesses-depression

21 Godberg, Joseph, M.D., reviewer, Drugs That Caused Depression http://www.webmd.com/depression/guide/medicines-cause-depression (May 2012), retrieved August 19, 2013

22 Seligman, M., *Flourish: A Visionary New Understanding of Happiness and Well-Being*. New York: Free Press (2011).

23 Seligman, M., *What You Can Change . . . and What You Can't*. New York: Random House (2006).

24 Tedeschi, R.G., Calhoun L.G., *Facilitating Post-Traumatic Growth: A Clinician's Guide*. Mahwah, NJ: Erlbaum (1999).

25 "Medicines that Cause Depression," (2011), Retrieved June 4, 2012, from http://www.webmd.com/depression/guide/medicines-cause-depression.

26 Tan., S.Y., Ortberg, J. *Coping with Depression*. Grand Rapids: Baker Books (2004).

27   Centre for Addiction and Mental Health. "Culture And Depression." ScienceDaily. ScienceDaily, 15 July 2008. <www.sciencedaily.com/releases/2008/07/080715071401.htm>. Retrieved February 16, 2014.

28   Hart, A., *Unmasking Male Depression*. Nashville, Thomas Nelson (2001).

29   Seligman, M., *Flourish: A Visionary New Understanding of Happiness and Well-Being*. New York: Free Press (2011).

30   S.A. Glied and R.G. Frank, "Shuffling Towards Parity: Bringing Mental Health Care Under the Umbrella," New England Journal of Medicine 359 (2008): 113-115; C.L. Barry, R.G. Frank and T.G. McGuire, "The Cost of Mental Health Parity: Still an Impediment?" Health Affairs 25 (2006), 623-34.

31   C. King and L.N.P. Voruganti, "What's in a Name? The Evolution of the Nomenclature of Antipsychotics Drugs," Journal of Psychiatry & Neuroscience 27 (2007).

32   Seligman, M., *Flourish: A Visionary New Understanding of Happiness and Well-Being*. New York: Free Press (2011).

33   Ibid.

34   Reivich, Karen, (2009). Resilience Training: Student Guide. Adapted by the U.S. Army, 34.

35   J.C. Loehlin, R.R. McCrae, and P.T. Costa, "Heritabilities of Common and Measure-Specific Components of the Big Five Personality Factors," Journal of Research in Personality 32 (1998), 431-53

36   http://www.nami.org/template_eoy.cfm?ContentID=146359&Section=not_alone&template=/ContentManagement/ContentDisplay.cfm, Retrieved August 19, 2013

37   http://www.nami.org/template_eoy.cfm?Section=not_alone&template=/ContentManagement/ContentDisplay.cfm&ContentID=146359 Retrieved February 17, 2014

38   Lyubomirky, S., Sheldon, K.M., and Schkade, D. "Pursuing Happiness; The architecture of sustainable change," (2005), Review of General Psychology, 111-131.

About John Thurman

John is a New Mexican with a Georgia accent. He and his wife Angie have lived in the Land of Enchantment more than twenty-five years.

John has a full time out-patient counseling practice that is affiliated with Christian Therapy Services in Albuquerque. In addition, John provides counseling, coaching, and consulting services both in person and via internet. John brings a unique perspective to direct sales business owners as he and his wife have been involved in the direct selling business for more than twenty-years.

John is also an international Crisis Response Specialist working with corporations, businessess as well as non-governmental agencies in the southwestern United States, Turkey, France, and the Middle East.

John has a Masters of Divinity degree from Southwestern Theological Seminary and a Masters of Counseling degree from Liberty University.

As a speaker, John delivers practical, researched-based information in a high energy, upbeat, and informative manner. John has been a trainer and speaker for Wells Fargo, Bank of America, The International Mission Board, Emcore Inc, Premier Designs Inc, Starbucks, LeFarge, The Blue Star Mom's, Ghost Ranch Writer's Conference, Presbyterian Health Plan, The North American Mission Board, The Navigators, and UPS.

He has written for Focus on the Family, The Albuquerque Journal's *Sage Women's* magazine. and *Christianity Today*.

He is a member of the New Mexico Counseling Association, the American Academy of Bereavement, the American Association of Christian Counselors, The International Christian Coaching Association, and the International Critical Incident Stress Foundation.

Follow John Thurman on

 John H. Thurman

 @johnthurman

Visit John's website and blog www.johnthurman.net

Bold Vision Books

PO Box 2011

Friendswood, Texas 77549

www.boldvisionbooks.com

For more information contact us at boldvisionbooks@gmail.com

Made in the USA
Charleston, SC
01 June 2014